Beyond the Darkness

Beyond the Darkness

My transforming Journey with Jesus

"I am the light of the world. Whoever follows me will not walk in darkness, but will have the light of life."

—*John 8:12*

Magdalene Patricia Balloy

Foreword by Father Michael Manning,
author of *The Fifteen Faces of God*

iUniverse, Inc.
New York Bloomington

Beyond the Darkness
My transforming Journey with Jesus

iUniverse books may be ordered through booksellers or by contacting:

iUniverse
1663 Liberty Drive
Bloomington, IN 47403
www.iuniverse.com
1-800-Authors (1-800-288-4677)

Because of the dynamic nature of the Internet, any Web addresses or links contained in this book may have changed since publication and may no longer be valid. The views expressed in this work are solely those of the author and do not necessarily reflect the views of the publisher, and the publisher hereby disclaims any responsibility for them.

ISBN: 978-1-4502-5689-6 (sc)
ISBN: 978-1-4502-5690-2 (dj)
ISBN: 978-1-4502-5691-9 (ebook)

Printed in the United States of America

iUniverse rev. date: 09/15/2010

Outline of Chapters

And a brief summary of the substance of the chronicles

Beyond the Darkness is a chronological and inspirational record of my life's journey with Christ, beginning with an out-of-body experience in 1963, when Jesus, in a glowing robe of pure light, appeared to me. *Beyond the Darkness* describes in detail all that has transpired in my daily walk with Jesus since that phenomenal experience and relates everything of substance in my life's journey, from the time of my birth on the island of Grenada, British West Indies, until the current time. These chronicles of my experiences, from the time I began to put it all together until this present date, cover a span of about forty years.

Introduction contains my notes of appreciation, a brief description of the substance of the book, and an explanation of why it was written.

Chapter 1: Born Again describes my phenomenal death experience, when Jesus appeared to me during a serious illness, and all that transpired after my recovery.

Chapter 2: Life's Journey Continues explains how God's Holy Spirit gradually took over my life to help me to grow into a healthy, happy, and productive woman of God.

Chapter 3: My Family shares my experiences as a wife and mother and relates the difficulties my husband and I encountered in raising our three children. Included in this chapter are some family photos.

Chapter 4: My Life gives a more complete description of my sad childhood experiences on the island of Trinidad, British West Indies, and relates the hardships my two brothers and I endured through the abuse of my alcoholic stepfather. There are also some pictures of me and my brothers in our youth.

Chapter 5: A Special Message shares my deep feelings of God's unconditional love and my belief that all of God's children can enter into His Holy Presence, to encounter for themselves their own life-changing love experience as they grow in the light of Christ, to bear fruit to His perfecting love.

Chapter 6: Dreams and Experiences with God relate some of my most unforgettable dreams. It explains how God's Holy Spirit teaches us through dreams, instructs us through proverbs, and how through faith and prayer He directs us in all aspects of our lives.

Chapter 7: Visions narrates my encounter with Christ through visions in my daily meditation, as Jesus led me into His Heavenly Kingdom.

Chapter 8: Introduction to Peter shares my experiences with Jesus through a vision, as He introduces me to Saint Peter.

Chapter 9: Challenges in Marriage details some of the difficulties my husband Art and I encountered in our marriage because of the differences in our personalities and beliefs.

Chapter 10: A Vision of Hope shares a vision I experienced in church while praying about whether or not I should return home to Art and continue our marriage.

Chapter 11: Recalling Our Beginning is a romantic and captivating recollection of how Art and I met, and how he pursued me, until I said yes to his proposal of marriage.

Chapter 12: Climbing a Mountain in Our Relationship explains some of the obstacles Art and I confronted in our long journey together as husband and wife. But through prayer, love, and forgiveness, our marriage survived for forty-eight years.

Chapter 13: A New Awakening details the ups and downs in our lives, not only in our marriage, but also in business. Yet, through all my daily frustrations, Jesus was the light that led me out of my own darkness.

Chapter 14: My Baptism in Light describes a transforming experience that took three days to realize. Through that vision I was shown the constraint of my own soul and my *nothingness* compared to Jesus.

Chapter 15: Called to Be Transformed relates an interesting vision, wherein

I observed my own spiritual transformation. Then Jesus led me to a table and instructed me to eat the meat of His flesh. Afterward, Jesus took me, and my husband Art, and presented us to His Heavenly Father.

Chapter 16: Call to Obedience tells how a voice spoke to me at four in the morning and instructed me to get out of bed and read Galatians. It also relates all that transpired after that experience and how I was "called to obedience."

Chapter 17: My Commission shares my belief about God's unconditional love for all people and my conviction that He has commissioned me, through the pages of this book, to bring others into a better understanding of His unconditional love.

Chapter 18: Christ Is Our Robe of Righteousness explains how, as we walk with Jesus, we are transformed into His image and likeness. Thus, we are protected by His light and have nothing to fear from Satan.

Chapter 19: A New Revelation relates a vision I experienced in church the Sunday after I completed "A Note to the Readers," which I intended to be the last chapter in this book. However, as always, God had another plan. Thus, I included this chapter before the final chapter.

Chapter 20: A Note to Readers is my prayer and farewell statement.

Epilogue articulates all that has transpired since the completion of the manuscript twenty years ago, and explains in detail the reason it took so long to get it published.

Conclusion explains why I decided to self-publish after returning from a six-day retreat in Omaha, Nebraska, in 2009.

Dedication

The Son of Mary is God's child of hope.
He came into the world as a star to follow.
His light shines bright for all to see.
So that our world may be transformed by His example of love and humility.

I dedicate this book to Jesus, God's pure light in this world!

My soul proclaims the greatness of the Lord;
My spirit rejoices in God my Savior.
For he has looked upon his handmaid's lowliness;
Behold from now on all ages will call me blessed.
The Mighty one has done great things for me,
And holy is his name.

—Luke 1:46–49

Acknowledgments

I thank God for Jesus' mother, Mary. God so loved her that He filled her with His Holy Spirit. Because of her, Jesus was born of the flesh. My prayer is that, through Jesus, all people may come into the presence of God the Father and that all will assimilate Mary, in total surrender to God's Holy Spirit, so that the Spirit of God's unconditional love will transform the face of the earth.

I must also thank my husband, Art, and my mother, Rosa. Though they are no longer with us on earth, they live with me in the spirit of love.

Additional thanks must be extended to every member of my entire family and all the special people I have had the good fortune to know throughout my life. Because of all of you, I have come to be the person that I am. Had you not been there for me on life's long journey and struggles, a very important element in my unfolding spiritual growth would be missing. I thank you for your love, your understanding, and for all constructive criticism that has helped me along the way.

To my kind friend Dolly Dorsey—there are no words that can effectively convey my gratitude to Dolly for all the time and effort she has put forth in the original preparation of this book. Without her loving response to my plea for help, this book might never have been ready for publication.

My appreciation continues to Dennis, my son, who transferred what Dolly had typed into his computer and took the time to teach me how to use it.

Thanks also go to Scott Williams, who gave me his old computer and spent a day transferring the manuscript from Dennis' computer into it, so that I could continue my work on this book.

My appreciation is also extended to Sunny Kreis Collins, author of *Kill the Clock*, for the initial editing of *Beyond the Darkness*.

And to Sister Maria Eva Moreno, for proof reading *Beyond the Darkness* before the final version was resubmitted to the publisher.

I pray God's blessings upon all of you! May you be filled with His eternal joy and peace! Your faithfulness, generosity, and giving of your precious time, unselfishly, has helped this unworthy servant with the task of putting His book together. I'm confident that, because of your support and encouragement, His unconditional love will shine through the pages of this book and touch the hearts of all who are open to His message of love.

Foreword

Beyond the Darkness is an honest, and sometimes embarrassing, exposure of Magdalene Balloy—wife, mother, and mystic.

We are overwhelmed by her stark humility, as she struggles to know, love, and be faithful to the people in her life.

We feel her pain as she faces abandonment as a child. We relate to her as she reaches out in love to her husband, Art, who battles with his own insecurities and fears.

The story of her relationship with her daughter and two sons is especially poignant. Her love is fragile, but overpowering.

She embraces the pain of her struggles through the intimacy she has with Jesus. In the midst of her rejection and confusion, Christ comes to her in visions of love, strength, and hope.

Magdalene's courageous revelation of joys and separations in her life helps us to face the suffering of our own lives.

Her words and poetry take us by the hand to show us we're not alone. We, too, can have the support of Jesus.

Beyond the Darkness shares the pain and victory of Magdalene's indomitable life.

Father Michael Manning, SVD
Wordnet Production
(Sharing God's love through media)
Author of *The Fifteen Faces of God*

Magdalene's Reflection

Beyond the Darkness!

Life at times seems like an endless journey in a vast wilderness of darkness.
Yet, beyond life's struggles and sadness
There is a nourishing garden of eternal bliss;
And all who achieve admittance to that garden
Reflect its radiant beauty.
For that is the garden of God's purest light.
How do I know?
I have glimpsed into that garden and was enchanted by its light;
Thus, I will not rest until I am completely out of this miserable place of
darkness.
I know that as long as I keep moving in the direction of God's pure light,
I will eventually come upon its source.
Then my soul will absorb its purifying rays!
So those who are near me and are approaching the garden of bliss
Will see a reflection of its pure light—shining through me!

Introduction

Now this is the message we have heard from Him
And proclaim to you
God is light, and in Him, there is no darkness at all.

—*1 John 1:5*

We are all called by God to share with everyone the good news of His unconditional love. *Beyond the Darkness* is a record of the experiences in my life, which have led me out of my own darkness and ignorance into the nourishing light of God's love. Because I now walk daily in the light of Christ, I can plainly see the pain and sufferings of others, as they, too, struggle on their own journeys through life. Consequently, I'm moved by compassion to share my story. I hope that somehow God's unconditional love will reach out and touch the hearts of all who read *Beyond the Darkness*, so that they, too, might see beyond their own struggles and sadness.

My life changed gradually after I experienced God's love through a deathlike occurrence, when Jesus appeared to me. That phenomenal experience inspired me to move in a new direction, with a positive approach to life. Since that memorable night, more than forty years ago, Jesus has been with me every step of the way, through good and bad times. Before I entered into His light, however, I was locked in a cold, dark place, filled with resentment, hatred, and self-pity. I felt lost, alone, and abandoned by God. Life for me did seem "like an endless journey in a vast wilderness of darkness." Jesus, nonetheless, has opened my eyes to the truth. Now I know that, beyond the darkness of life's drudgery, there is a beautiful garden within the depths of every human soul. And all who enter into that garden are transformed by God's love. For that's where God lives. That place is referred to by Jesus as "The Kingdom Within."

In order to find that heavenly place, we must follow Jesus, for He is the pure light of God. His light is only light that can lead us there. Jesus is the reason and purpose for this book. I would have nothing of any value to write about had it not been for Jesus coming into my life. The changes that took place in me were slow and sometimes very painful. It was a growing process, which is never easy. I had to grow in understanding of myself, the meaning of life, and the value of God's Word in the Holy Scriptures. Gradually but surely, my life began to change, as Jesus became my constant companion. As I walked with Jesus, through daily prayer and meditation, He began to teach me about myself and God's Kingdom.

Now He has commissioned me to share with the world all He has shown and taught me through my daily experiences. The writing of this book is by far the most difficult task I have ever had to accomplish. You will understand why after reading the complete book. Yet, I have been faithful to His command. It has taken me over forty years to put it all together. The reason for the delay is explained in full detail in the epilogue.

When I first experienced the true warmth of God's unconditional love in my life, I wanted to share my feelings with the world. I began to write poetry and shared my poems with anyone and everyone who would stand still long enough to listen. My friends would say to me; "Madelene, that's beautiful! Why don't you put your poems in a little book, so that more people can enjoy them?" That was the original purpose for this book. But, as I began to put my poems together, Jesus took over my life and began to instruct me through visions and dreams—which I share in detail throughout the book, but especially in the chapters on visions and dreams. I hope that you will enjoy reading the details of my life's journey in every chapter; in reading my story, you will be blessed, because, without Jesus' instructions, there would be no book.

It's with the Lord that I now move, live, and have my existence. Because of Jesus, I have entered into the presence of God the Father; consequently, I am commanded to share the good news: *"God is light, and in Him there is no darkness"* (1 John, 1:5). Yes! Christ is all around us, and God's beauty is everywhere. The road we travel in life, however, is sometimes steep and narrow. Nevertheless, with Jesus at my side, I am no longer afraid, because I am secure in Him. Psalm 23 relates my deep feelings perfectly.

Because the Lord is my shepherd, I have everything I need!
He lets me rest in the meadow grass and leads me beside the quiet streams.
He restores my failing health.
He helps me do what honors him the most.
Even when walking through the dark valley of death I will not be afraid,
For you are close beside me, guarding, guiding all the way.
You provide delicious food for me in the presence of my enemies.
You have welcomed me as your guest; blessings overflow!
Your goodness and unfailing kindness shall be with me all of my life.
And afterwards I will live with you forever in your home.

—Psalm 23:1–6

Since my encounter with Jesus, I have developed a hungering desire to express myself through poetry. *Beyond the Darkness* relates my life experiences and confirms through visual detailing (and sometimes through poetry) how my walk with Jesus transformed me and helped me to discover God's beautiful garden within myself. *Beyond the Darkness* is meant to give praise to Jesus. I dedicate all that I write to Him.

Most gracious Heavenly Father, we thank you for sending Jesus into the world to show us the way back to You. Help us to learn all that we need to learn each day from Him, so that He, working through us, may change our lives and transform our world. Open our spiritual eyes, so that we may see things as You see them; teach us humility and meekness, so that we may totally surrender to the loving presence of Your Holy Spirit. Soften our hearts, and heal our memories of all deep hurts, so that we may truly be able to love and forgive as You, Father, command us to love and forgive. And, Father, please remove all darkness from each soul, so that all people might live again, in your Holy Presence, here on this earth and in Your eternal garden of light. We ask all this, in the holy name of Jesus, Your Son, our beloved Brother and Savior. Amen

1

BORN AGAIN

For if we have grown in union with him
Through a death like his,
We shall also be united with him in the resurrection.

—*Romans 6:5*

The cold, dark night of life began for me at my birth on the island of Grenada, British West Indies, in the year 1932. When I was five, Trinidad, West Indies, became my home, where I lived until I was nineteen. At that age, I moved to California, and I have lived in California ever since. Now, however, I also live in God's Kingdom, and I draw my nourishment from His unconditional love.

I have, indeed, experienced sadness in my life. It began for me at an early age. In my childhood, as far back as I can remember, there were few, if any, happy days. My childhood was filled with illness, the unhappiness of a broken home, and poverty. Because of all these hardships, and many more, too numerous to mention, my formal schooling did not exceed the eighth grade; consequently, living was not easy. Pessimism plagued my soul, which made me think that life was not worth the struggle. My negative disposition and constant preoccupation with self-pity made it exceedingly difficult for me to really enjoy life. However, at the age of thirty, I had an experience that transformed me completely. I do not mean to imply that life is all sunshine now, or that the incident has brought material wealth. It has, however, inspired me in the attainment of something that is of far greater value than material wealth. Now the challenges of each new day have become an opportunity for growth—my eyes have been opened to my own imperfections, so that I can readily forgive the imperfections of others. Through these past years, I have learned to accept myself for who I am yet still strive to grow and unfold to the best of my inherent ability. By surrendering my life to God, I know that He is teaching me and showing me how.

In April 1963 I was very ill; I had been since January. My illness began with the mumps, which served to weaken my resistance. I caught all flu in season that year. Because of the flu, I contracted a serious lung infection, in conjunction with an accelerated heart rate. That condition made the simple function of breathing for me a very arduous task. In fact, one night, after a most miserable day, I went to bed feeling as though my time had come—although at that particular moment, I was not yet ready to die.

My three children, Michael, Dennis, and Noelle Rose, who are all grown now, were quite young then and were not yet self-sufficient. At that time my children were my only real joy in life. The love I felt for them filled me with sadness at the thought of leaving them motherless. My sadness gave way to tears, and, as tears flowed, I prayed to God from deep within my heart, asking His forgiveness for all the times I had wished to die, pleading with Him to spare my life for the sake of my children.

I also prayed to the Blessed Mother, begging her to ask Jesus to make me well again, convinced in my mind that the Blessed Mother would really understand exactly how I felt about leaving my helpless children in such a cruel world. While praying, I drifted off into what *seemed* to be a restful sleep. Suddenly, I felt as though I had died! I saw my soul come out of my body, and I sat up in bed, while my body was still lying down. The room was dark, but instantly, a soft light penetrated the darkness. At the foot of my bed, a transparent figure of Jesus appeared, in a glowing robe of pure light. The light that radiated from Him made the night look like dawn. I could plainly see my entire bedroom and everything in it, including my husband, Art, who was sound asleep in the same bed, next to my lifeless body.

Jesus stood silently there, at the foot of my bed, with His arms outstretched in front of Him, as if beckoning my soul to come forth. An unforgettable feeling of peace and true bliss engulfed me. As the burdens of life were lifted from me, I knew that all my sins were forgiven and that the time had indeed come for me to depart from this earth. I tried to speak but had no voice. In thought I said, *No Lord! Please let me stay. I don't want to go yet.* With that thought, my soul immediately returned to my body. Instantaneously, Jesus was gone. The room was dark, and I was again afraid. Days passed; my illness worsened. A week later I was hospitalized. While in the hospital, I could not sleep; I was convinced that death was near. My mind was consumed with prayers, repenting, and pleading with God for forgiveness and renewed life. After ten days, my temperature returned to normal. On the eleventh day, I was discharged from the hospital in an improved condition.

When I returned home from the hospital, my whole attitude changed.

I became aware of all my numerous blessings. In appreciation for this new awareness, I thanked God for bringing me to the realization that life is, indeed, worthwhile. When I recovered, a very different person emerged. It was like being "born again" with new insight, which made me aware of God's marvelous artistry and the wonders that He has created all around us.

Since then, through my intuitive observation of nature, I have discovered the true value of life. Now the breathtaking beauty of an early sunrise, the boundless energy of the ocean tide, and the meticulous orchestration of the universe provide me with inspiration and a zealous enthusiasm for life. Yes! I have become a true student of life, constantly investigating its mysteries. In these past forty plus years, I have read numerous books on the life of Jesus, His disciples, and the saints, as well as books that are scientific and philosophical; all of my readings were educational. The knowledge gained from my search confirmed my belief in God. In my quest for truth, I discovered God within myself. Now I know that God is the miraculous substance of life. He can be found within every human heart. And His face can be seen in the midst of nature. In consequence, my mind has acquired peace with itself. Jesus led me out of the darkness of ignorance and into His Father's Kingdom. That's where I live now, because I have found my home in Him.

The Storms of Life

Yes, indeed, I have come to realize
The storms of life are nature's way of nourishing us,
And that everyone is an essential part of God's family tree.
Therefore, we all have the innate ability to grow.
All we need is a real desire to do so.
For when a desire sets one's heart aflame,
The intensity of that fire, when it is contained,
Is like a nuclear-powered device
That can thrust man out of his limited environment
Into God's vast territory!

More than forty years have passed since my phenomenal death experience. Through those years, I have weathered many storms—because I knew it did not matter how bleak the day seemed, the sun was shining somewhere, and it would come out again, if not tomorrow, then in the very near future. During that period of time, I was pushed and shoved by a hungering need to express myself in poetry. Sometimes, at the most frustrating moments in my life, I was moved by the greatest inspiration to write. However, putting my thoughts into words on paper was never an easy task, because often the words that would flow into meaningful poetry were words that I could not spell. Nevertheless, by the power of God's Holy Spirit, and with the help of Webster's Dictionary, I have overcome that obstacle.

After Jesus appeared to me, I embarked on a very extensive self-improvement program, which is ongoing and never-ending. Consequently, I began to read every book I could find that would help me with that task. In one of those early books, *Psycho-Cybernetics*, by Dr. Maxwell Maltz, Dr. Maltz suggested to readers that after reading it they write down on paper how they felt his book had helped them. He also suggested they write an affirmation on what they would like to accomplish in their lives. So, with pencil and paper in hand, I began to write. When I was through, I had written my very first poem, entitled: "A Life Worthwhile."

A Life Worthwhile

I want my life to be worthwhile.
I don't want time to pass me by,
To live a little every day,
And learn a lot in every way
That's what I want to do each day
To make my life worthwhile.
I'll start each day this thought in mind
"I will do those things designed
To make me best in every way
So that my desire will always stay,
To make my life worthwhile."
So when at last my time has come
I could say to those around
"I have lived my life the fullest way!
I have no regrets at all this day,
For I have lived a life worthwhile.

I have, indeed, been trying to live that affirmation. Yet, it is not always easy to follow through on one's affirmation. Life is full of ups and downs. But I have learned to roll with the fall and to always get up to start over again—and again. Now I seem to fall less with every new step, as I get nearer to the top of God's Holy Mountain. Though life is difficult, I have come this far because Jesus is always at my side, comforting me with His loving touch and picking me up with lasting words of encouragement. After the appearance of Jesus in my life, I felt so alive I wanted to share my feelings of joy with the world. I wrote the story "Born Again" in 1972 and submitted it to the Reader's Digest first-person story department. It was returned to me unpublished.

At that time, Art had been out of work for more than six months, recovering from a back injury. We had very little to live on. In those early days of our marriage, I was just a wife and mother with no income of my own, so we were really hoping that my story would be published; any extra money would have been a great help to our family's financial difficulties. However, it was not the will of God for it to be published at that time. After the rejection from Reader's Digest, we decided that writing was not my forte and agreed that I should go out and get a job to help out financially. Therefore, in 1973, after being a homemaker and mother for eighteen years, I had to go back to work. My first job was at Robinsons Department Store, which later became Robinsons-May Company. I worked there for ten years in sales, and I continued to work outside the home, in sales, for almost thirty years.

In 2004, I had to quit working because of Art's failing health. After his death, in April of that same year, I did go back to work for a short period of time. But my heart was not in working for a living. I wanted to work at building God's Kingdom here on earth.

Since Art's death, I have become very involved in my church, in various ministries. I am a chairwoman in Our Lady's Desert Roses, the Palm Desert chapter of Magnificat, A Ministry to Catholic Women. And I am an active volunteer on the Chaplaincy Team at Eisenhower Medical Center in Rancho Mirage. Thus, I'm still actively working, but not for money; now I'm "building my treasures in heaven."

Throughout those years of my working outside the home, however, I continued to grow and unfold daily in the light of Christ. My mind then, as it is now, was actively pursuing more knowledge about my spiritual self as well as life in general. My heart continues to seek God's providence in my present life. And, the desire to express God's unconditional love and peace to others still flows from me in the form of poetry, as well as in active church and hospital ministries

In 1981, the Catholic Renew program was initiated in my old parish in Woodland Hills. The Renew Program was established by the Catholic Church to bring parishioners together in small sharing groups to read Bible verses and to have discussions on how each person in the group felt about how God was working in his or her life.

Out of the Renew program prayer groups were formed: "reach-out" programs and other worthwhile community activities in each parish neighborhood. I participated in different small groups each semester for the duration of the three-year program in our church at Saint Bernardine's in Woodland Hills.

During the time of my participation in Renew, the Holy Spirit became very active in my life. The last segment of the Renew program in that parish was on the gifts of the Holy Spirit. We talked about how we should allow the Holy Spirit to work through us for the good of the whole community.

This book is the result of a new awakening that took place in me because of the Renew program; that program brought me to the realization that we must completely surrender our lives to Jesus, so that His Holy Spirit can bear fruit in us. I will share more about bearing God's spiritual fruit in chapter five.

Born Again
The darkness of ignorance filled me with unhappiness
For the first thirty-five years of my life.
But at last the long, cold night has passed.
God sent His Son to penetrate the darkness of my soul.
His light was so warm and bright it melted the snow
So that the seed within could grow;
And His love brought the dawn of a new day.

2

LIFE'S JOURNEY CONTINUES

There are different kinds of spiritual gifts but the same spirit;
There are different forms of service but the same Lord;
There are different workings but the same God
Who produces all of them in everyone!

—*1 Corinthians 12:4–6*

Because the gifts of the Holy Spirit are to be shared with the whole community, I share my experiences with you now, hoping that, through the power of the Holy Spirit, a change may be initiated in you. That is, of course, if you feel there is something missing in your life. Before the Renew program came into our parish, I knew that God was working in my life, and I gave Him thanks for all His blessings. In spite of that, I felt a deep need to do more than to just give thanks. God was calling me to do more, but at that time I really did not know what He wanted me to do.

During our discussions in Renew on the gifts of the Holy Spirit, I came to realize that God had bestowed on me a special gift of communication. He wants me to share with you, to spread the good news about His unconditional love, and to relate to you everything He has shown and taught me about life—and to remind you of your special place in His heart. It does not matter who you are or where you are at this very moment in time. You might be in a cold, dark place or off on a cloud somewhere; wherever you are, He is there with you. We all have the gift of free will, so we can turn our backs on God anytime. But He is never far from us and can always reach us. However, because we do have a free will, God must have our permission to help us find our way back to Him.

There are many people seeking God who have searched for Him but cannot seem to find Him. Because they cannot find God, they say, "God does not exist." And there are others who think that God will have nothing to do with them, because they do not feel worthy to approach Him. I can relate to those who feel they are not worthy to approach God, because that's exactly how I felt before Jesus came into my life. Jesus, however, is approachable. He is our oldest brother and friend—our Savior, who came into a darkened world to lead all who are lost and disheartened back into His Father's beautiful garden of light. That garden is the place of eternal peace, joy, and love—of blissful harmony between and among all of His creation. That place is called God's Kingdom. Everyone who lives there knows God. He is the center of their lives. If you are interested in finding that heavenly place, go to Jesus. Jesus will give you all the information you need to lead you to God. But go to Jesus with an open mind and a humble heart. When our minds are closed, it's impossible to be humble. If we believe we have all the answers, we close ourselves off from God. People like that will never find God. There are so many lost souls today who believe that there is no God and believe that they owe nothing to anyone. They also believe that when they die existence for them will just end. They live in what they call "the real world" and believe in only what they can see. Those who believe in only what they can see have a big surprise awaiting them. I highly recommend a book by Lincoln Barnett entitled *The Universe and Dr. Einstein*. It's a very old book, published in March 1952 by Signet Science Library. Mr. Barnett explains in this book Einstein's Theory of Relativity, in a manner that is completely comprehensible even to me. That book helped me to understand that most of what exists in the universe cannot be seen with just the naked eye.

Because God cannot be seen with our human eyes does not mean that He does not exist. To find God, we must look within our hearts and search the depths of our souls, for God is the life within us. Without God, there would be no life. Everything in the universe comes from God, and all must return to Him. That is the reason why so many people feel frustrated and lost—because they are looking for God in all the wrong places. And some do not really know what is missing in their lives; they only know that something is missing. I was one of those who felt that something was missing in my life. Even after I found God, there were still feelings of emptiness in me. It was not until I totally surrendered my life to Him and emptied myself of "self" that He was able to fill me with His Holy Spirit. Now the emptiness is gone. God's Holy Spirit lives in me. He sustains and comforts me. His love fills my heart. And now I have been commissioned by Him to share my life with others and to touch them with His love. The poem, "Let His Light Shine" explains my deep feelings. I wrote this poem in 1986 and sent it out to my friends and family that Christmas. This poem is my new affirmation, because

I truly believe that Jesus is calling me, and all persons of faith, to be His light of love in this sad, dark world.

Let His Light Shine!

I want to sing, dance, laugh, and play to show my joy in every way.
I want to share my life with others, too
And be happy in all that I do.
I want to reach out and touch the world, to start a fire where hearts are cold
I want to warm those hearts in such a way that they will feel God's love each day.
I want to tell the world that God's love is true.
It depends not on what we do.
For God is patient, forgiving, and kind.
He waits for us to change our minds
So that we may learn and come to know
His love is the light that makes an angel glow.
I want to be the Christ that everyone can see
So that the world will know that Jesus has transformed me.
I want to be a lamp, from which His Light shines.
So that everyone will know His love is mine.
I want to tell the world that Jesus is theirs to hold.
So embrace one another, take a chance, and be bold!
Jesus is our brother, our sister, a wife, and husband, too.
He dwells within our midst and sees everything we do.
So Christmas will forever be a day to celebrate
It's the time of year that reminds us: our Father's love is great.
So, let Jesus into your life; His love will fill the air.
Then the world will see His light and know that He is near.
Yes! Let His love fill your heart.
It will transform your life in such a way
That peace and joy will flow from you.
To light your path each day!

3

MY FAMILY

Trust in the Lord
With all your heart,
On your own intelligence rely not.
In all your ways be mindful of Him,
And He will make straight your paths.

—*Proverbs 3:5–6*

Picture of my family in church:(Left to right) Dennis, Noelle, Art and Madelene, Michael and Janet, Rosa and Charles Mitchelson, on the occasion of the twenty-fifth wedding anniversary of my mother and her third husband, Charles Mitchelson.

In every family there are disagreements and arguments, even in a loving family. Our family was no different. Our daughter, Noelle Rose, and I were very close when she was a child, and until she was sixteen we continued to be very good friends. I thought she was an angel sent to me from heaven. Noelle, at a very young age showed her intelligence, kindness, lovingness, and compassion for others; she seemed to have a deep understanding about philosophical things. To me, she was like a ray of sunlight that brightened my days. But, at the age of sixteen, Noelle lost her wings and fell flat on her face. At the age of sixteen, her attitude changed. At that very young age, she wanted to be totally independent and did not want to be told what she could or could not do. I really don't understand what went wrong in our relationship. Nevertheless, in reflecting back now, I can see that was the onset of a very dark road that Noelle eventually took to separate herself from our family. The poem "My Noelle Rose" describes the way I saw her at the age of eleven.

My Noelle Rose

Was born on the twenty-fourth at night
She is my Christmas delight.
Her fragrance is divine.
She is more refreshing than springtime.
To me she is the sweetest flower that grows.
My Noelle Rose,
Is becoming more beautiful as she unfolds
With golden brown hair; and glasses on her nose
She dances about on her toes.
She also likes to sing and read
And would help anyone in need
Though Noelle is my little star,
She outshines me by far.
She's thoughtful, generous, and kind.
A truer friend you'll never find.
Noelle is my youngest "gem" of three
and is a precious part of me.
She is the essence of my life.
And soon she will be shining bright
Then the entire world will see,
She's an important part of God's family tree

At the age of twenty, Noelle completely separated herself from us and everyone connected to her childhood and youth. I pray for her daily, knowing that she is in God's care and that Jesus will show her the way back into His light. I have endured much heartache in my life; however, being severed from Noelle has been the most painful. For more than two years we did not know where she was. In May of 1995 she sent me a Mother's Day card, and she telephoned us on Thanksgiving Day that same year. Then she withdrew herself again from us. For several years we did not hear from her or know her whereabouts. After we had not heard from her in about three years, one year she sent us a Christmas card and her post office box address. For many years we would write to her at that address. But she would not respond to our mail. In spite of that, I continued to write to her whenever the spirit moved me. About a year before Art died, she contacted her brother Dennis by e-mail. So they were in touch with each other. Since Art's death, Noelle and I have been corresponding with each other by e-mail. I sent the following poem to Noelle during the time when we did not hear from her.

My Only Daughter

You are my only daughter and always will be,
Yet, you are in a place so far away from me.
If only I could see your face
And feel the warmth of your embrace
Life for me would be complete again.
For although I'm your only mother
I would also like to be your friend.

When Noelle was away at school, I was asked to write a letter that would be presented to her by the women's committee at her university. They were holding a special evening for all the young ladies who were attending that school. That special evening was entitled, A Tribute to Womanhood. My letter had to say something to Noelle that would be an inspiration to her and a tribute to womanhood. Below is the letter that I wrote to her then.

> Noelle darling,
> Although I am unable to be with you in person this evening, my love is there with you in spirit. What can I say that would be meaningful to you now about womanhood? You were a delightful and beautiful child, who brought much joy into my life. You were like a spark of sunlight shining through the darkness of my life. And now that you are a woman, your beauty is visible for all to see. That inner spark still shines through and will continue to shine

13

until you become the perfect light that God intended you
to be; a light that will shine into the world as a tribute
to womanhood. I know not what direction your life will
take, but I am sure that you will put forth every effort into
being the very best person that is within you to be.

You know as well as I that women are very important
to the world. I believe that women are favored in God's
eyes. All things in nature come from Mother Earth. Thus,
as the earth is important to all living things, so, too, are
women. Women are the womb of the earth, and as such
we have an obligation to guide, teach, and inspire. If we
turned our backs on our responsibilities, the world would
be a sad, dark place. So, bring forth your light into the
world so that all who are near you may feel the warmth of
its glow. And as they are touched by that light, their lives
will be nourished.

I love you very much and always will. God blessed
me with you. And He blessed you with a unique
gift of understanding. Let that gift shine through in
your relationships with others, so that your ability to
understand will be a guiding light for all to follow. When
Jesus said, "You are the light of the world," He was
speaking to everyone about that "pure inner light" that
so few of us will ever see. But, as long as you continue to
move in the direction of that light, you will eventually
come upon its source. Then your life will be brightened
in such a way that others will draw warmth from it. Then
you'll be the kind of woman God intended you to be, and
you will be a tribute, to womanhood.

After rereading that letter, I wept. I felt God was also speaking to me, as
He is now speaking to every woman who reads this book.

Noelle started experiencing dizzy spells at the age of sixteen. She had
every known test that was available at that time from the best medical centers
in Los Angeles. But no one could find the cause of her problem. She continued
to suffer from dizzy spells throughout high school and her time away at
college. However, she seemed to be coping with it, and so were we. Noelle
moved back to California before graduating college, because we were no
longer financially able to help her continue her education in an out-of-state
university. We all agreed that she would finish her schooling at California
State University at Northridge.

About six months after Noelle had returned to California, her dizziness worsened and put an end to her ability to support herself. Noelle moved back home with us. Her doctors thought that she might have multiple sclerosis. When Noelle told us what they were checking her for, I went into a tailspin, and our family was devastated! Now we know that Noelle's dizziness was not caused by multiple sclerosis. The last test at UCLA Medical Center positively confirmed that it was not MS. What she did have at that time was a drinking problem. Alcohol became a part of Noelle's life from the time she entered high school. We were not aware of her problem, because her grades were never affected by her drinking. We suspect now that alcoholism and drugs were two of the main reasons for her separation from us. I could write a whole book about all that we have gone through with Noelle, but I will only relate what I believe the Holy Spirit wants me to share with you. Through my recent correspondence with Noelle by e-mail, I know that she is still having some serious health problems. She has a neurological disorder yet I believe that God is working in Noelle's life and that He will heal her and again put her life in order. I continue to pray for her daily, trusting God for her welfare.

Our two sons, Michael and Dennis, have always felt that Noelle got all the attention. Noelle was a very invigorating child, and she would put a lot of effort into everything she did. She always brought home excellent grades. Not only was she a good student, but she had many interests. She took dance, music, and art lessons. She was a Girl Scout, and she sang in our church. She was in her high school marching band and in the school orchestra; she was also involved in many other school activities. Noelle received numerous awards for her accomplishments as a student. Of course she got our attention!

Art and I were not the kind of parents who would force their children to take extra lessons outside of school work or to involve them in activities in which they were not interested. Michael and Dennis were exposed to everything in the same way that Noelle was, but they were just not interested. Dennis, our middle son, felt lost in the shuffle. He had a very difficult time in school and needed help to cope with the situation. We got Dennis the help he needed, and he graduated from high school. But Dennis did not want to go to college. During high school Dennis worked with Art in our construction business. He still works in construction and has his own home and recently got married. Dennis is extremely intelligent and has a lot to contribute to society. Unfortunately, he is not yet aware of his God-given full potential. Dennis has suffered from depression off and on since grade school. His depression continues, and my prayers also continue. I ask God daily to help Dennis find contentment within himself, as he, too, learns to surrender completely to the light of Christ that's within him.

Michael, our oldest, got along all right in school until his last year. He started cutting classes then and almost did not graduate, but, by the grace of God, Michael graduated from high school with his classmates. We tried hard to encourage Michael to continue his education, but he would have no part of it. He said, "No way! I'm sick of school, and I'm not going to college." We told him, "Either you go to college, join the military service, or move out." So Michael moved out of our home, got a job, and moved into an apartment with a friend who was trying to make it on his own while attending college. After Michael moved out of our home, he started experimenting with drugs and was taking full advantage of his new freedom. One Sunday morning at 3:30 our doorbell was ringing "off the wall." Art hurried to the door to answer it. One of Michael's friends was standing there. He said, "Mr. Balloy, I'm sorry to have to tell you this, Michael had an accident, and we had to take him to the hospital." Can you imagine what state my mind was in with news like that at 3:30 in the morning? Michael had gone to the beach with friends that Saturday night. While crossing the highway to get back to his car, he was almost killed by a drunk driver. Thank God Michael's only serious injury was a broken leg.

While Michael was recuperating, he moved back into the house with us. He continued his experiments with drugs, even though he was now living at home. We had many discussions with Michael about the evils of drugs. Every discussion on that subject always ended in an argument from Michael and tears from me. Those were sad, dark days for us. But I continued daily to lift Michael up in prayer. When Michael was twenty-two, Janet came into his life, and what we were unable to do, Janet did. She got Michael to quit drugs. Michael married Janet when he was twenty-four. They are the parents of two daughters, Candace and Carli, who are grown women now and have families of their own. When I prayed for help with Michael, God sent Janet into our lives.

God is good. He always answers our heartfelt prayers…We are very fortunate to be blessed with so much. God provides everything we really need. He sent into my life a kind and caring husband and three beautiful souls for us to watch over when they were young. Now we also have Janet, and our two beautiful granddaughters, and at the present time I'm also a great-grandmother of three. Our life's journey together has not been easy; at times, I am difficult to live with—an angel I'm not, of that much I'm sure!

When Art and I married more than fifty years ago, I decided then that I would be the best wife I could be to him. Also, I told myself when we had children that I was going to be the best mother I could be. I have tried very hard to live up to those promises I made to myself. But I am positive that if you were to ask my family, they might think otherwise. What is best in the eyes of one person is not always best in the eyes of another. It depends on where we are, as we are looking at it.

The poem "Dear Family" was written at Christmas time in 1986. Art and I were going through a hard time financially. We had a family discussion about the problem, and it was suggested that we should refrain from exchanging gifts that Christmas. Our three children were all grown. Michael and Janet had their own family. Carli, the younger of our two granddaughters, had been born in August and was four months old that Christmas. Our first granddaughter, Candace, had been born in November of 1984. She was now two years old. Candace was having health problems. In November 1986, at Thanksgiving, Candace was in the hospital with pneumonia. Consequently, our family's greatest concern at that point was Candace's health, not how much we were going to spend on Christmas gifts.

In spite of all that was going on at that time, some members of our family (my mother especially) thought that Christmas without gifts was not Christmas. Christmas was my mother's favorite time of the year. She loved to give and receive presents. Everyone in my family always celebrated Christmas at our home in West Hills. Christmas Eve was the most enjoyable time for us, as it was also Noelle's birthday. We would invite all our friends over to our open house, to eat and sing Christmas carols, and to celebrate Noelle's birthday.

Christmas mornings, Art and I and our children would go to Mass and then come home to open our gifts. Christmas day was spent with our family. Michael and Janet would come over early, stay for the opening of the gifts, and then leave to spend the rest of the day with Janet's family. My mother, her husband, Charles, and Errol, my half brother, would come back to our home after we got back from church, to have breakfast with us and to open gifts.

That year, however, we wanted to move beyond just gift-giving and to focus our attention on the real meaning of Christmas. I did not do much shopping for Christmas presents that year; instead, I wrote the following poem and read it to my family at gift-opening time.

Dear Family

My special gift to each of you is me;
Please, look beyond what you see.
See with your heart, and let's start from here
To fill the New Year with joy that we can all share.
God loves us so much, He brought us together,
To learn from one another
And He sent Jesus into our lives to teach us how to live.

So let's follow Him; then we'll never go astray.
And let His spirit of love be born anew today
For I can surely see His face; He is sitting in your place.
Yes! I see Jesus in you, in all the nice things that you do.
Art, whenever we embrace, and there's a smile on your face,
And when you tell me that you care, it's His voice I hear
Yes! Darling, I know that your love is true,
Because I can see Jesus in you.
Dennis, I see Jesus in you, too, when you help me with my work
As often you do, and when you visited Grandma
In the hospital when she was ill.
You showed her that you cared; with her Jesus's love you then shared
That day He was at her bed.
Noelle, I have always seen Jesus in you.
When you were a child His joy filled your heart
And in you I could see His special spark.
Now that you are grown, when you share yourself with me
And tell me how you feel and show that you care,
As I share my feelings too,
Then I can surely feel His love coming through.
Michael, I see Jesus in you, through the love that you give
To your own family, when you work overtime to pay all the bills.
Then you cried on Thanksgiving, because Candace was ill;
Yes! I see Jesus in you.
Janet, I see Jesus in you, in the mother that you are
In the wife and person you are becoming
In the way that you have grown
And in the love for me you have shown
Yes I see Jesus in you.
Mom, I see Jesus in you in the way that you have suffered
When you were in pain, I could see His face
And I knew that He was hurting with you;
And whenever you are kind and thoughtful, too,
It's Jesus' love that shines from you.
Charles, I see Jesus in you, in how much you love Rosa
When she had surgery and you sat by her bed
I could tell that you were hurting with her
As you looked into her face, and, gently touched her head.
Errol, I see Jesus in you
As you're opening each package on Christmas day,
Filled with anticipation of what you will find;

The joy that you show is truly divine
Yes! I see Jesus in you.
And Jesus is waiting in the very same way, to open our hearts today.
He is our most precious gift, sent to us from our Father above.
He came to brighten our lives and to fill our hearts with love,
So I thank each and every one of you
Because of all that you do; His Spirit is here to stay;
Yes, I see Jesus in all of you. But,
I see Him in our neighbor, Irene, too.
I see Jesus in everyone I meet. And even the poor
People whose home is on the street;
Yes! I see Jesus, everywhere.
Because of Him, His Father's love I share
So when my time on earth has passed
And I'm in my heaven's home at last
I hope you'll remember me, not by what you now see
But you could truly speak of me and say,
"Madelene was not perfect in every way. But her heart was pure
It was filled with joy, because she loved."
Thus, this Christmas, my sincere wish for everyone is
That Jesus will continue to fill our hearts with joy
And that His love will transform our lives
To make us all happier: fathers, mothers, brothers, sisters,
Sons, daughters, husbands, and wives!
May God's love always shine from each and every one of us!
I love all of you in a very special way
Thus I want to share myself with you each day
Don't hold against me all the wrongs things that I do.
God's love is unconditional, and that's the way I love you.
Merry Christmas 1986

Art and me and our children: Michael has his arms around Art's neck. Dennis is in the middle, and Noelle is on my lap. This is at the ocean in Santa Monica, California, in 1960.

My mother, me, and our family pets at our old home in West Hills

This is our family at home, after church on Christmas Day 1965.

This picture of another Christmas shows Art and me.

4

My Life

God is our refuge and our strength
An ever-present help in our distress

—*Psalm 46:1*

The circumstances at the beginning of my life were most unfortunate. I came into the world out of wedlock. My mother later married a man who was not my father. He was an alcoholic who molested me as a child. When he was drunk, he would beat my mother, and if my brothers and I got in the way, he would also beat us. Mother left him when I was eight years old. She took me and my older brother, Alan, back to Grenada and left us there with relatives. Mother then went back to Trinidad to find work and a place for us to live, so that she could take care of us. Errol, my younger half brother, was two years old; he was left with his alcoholic father. When my brother, Alan, was seventeen, and I was sixteen, Mother came to the United States and left us with strangers. Errol was then ten years old and still lived with his father.

Mother left Trinidad for the United State in 1949 in order to marry Bill Henkel. Mother met Bill when he was in the military and stationed in Trinidad. Bill received his orders to return home before Mother's divorce was final. At that in time in Trinidad, there was a two-year waiting period before anyone could marry again after a divorce. Mother left us behind, because that was her only option. She fully intended to send for us as soon as she was able to do so. Unfortunately, it took her three years before she was able to save enough money to send for me. The United States Immigration Department wanted to be sure that I would not be a ward of the state.

The family that Alan and I were left to live with did not live by moral ethics. They were neighbors who lived next door to us. Mother was friendly with them and thought they were very kind to offer to take care of us until she was able to send for us. However, she did not really know these people as Alan and I got to know them when we lived with them. I felt as if we had been thrown into a snake pit with demons! Alan was very unhappy that Mother was gone. He got a job on a ship and left Trinidad, never to return. I was devastated. Alan and I had been very close as children. He had always defended me at school, or anyplace, for that matter. If anyone tried to hurt me, he would be right there for me. We did everything together and had such a good time! Other kids, who did not know us, thought that he was my boyfriend! After Alan left, I felt as though my world was crumbling. I was sinking into depression. Everyone I cared about had deserted me. I was extremely unhappy, so I prayed—and God answered my prayer.

A very kind and loving woman, who was a half sister of my mother's alcoholic husband, took pity on me and told me I could live with her. This kind and generous lady, who did not have much to live on herself, shared what little she did have with me. I continued to live with her until I came to California. This wonderful person who showed love to me was Olga Arthur. I am sure that God has rewards in Heaven for Olga because of her kindness toward me.

For many years we did not know where my brother Alan was or if he was still alive. The last time we saw him had been twenty-five years earlier, when he came to Los Angeles from Norway. The shipping company that he worked for had sent him to Los Angeles to replace someone who had gotten sick on one of their ships. Alan surprised us when he appeared on our driveway in a taxi. It had been ten years since we had last seen him. Alan spent the night with us and then left by ship for Norway the next day. We did not see Alan, nor did we hear from him, in all those years. Alan was very bitter. He resented our mother for leaving us in Trinidad with strangers. Alan had become a very heavy drinker and was trying to drown himself in alcohol.

Mother sent for Errol when he was sixteen. He lived with her and Bill Hinkle, her second husband, in California until he was eighteen. Then he left home and traveled around the United States for years, without any contact with us. Mother was concerned about his safety and worried constantly about his welfare. One day, after years of not knowing where he was, I received a letter from him. He was in a state mental hospital in northern California. His letter said: "I am in a place with a lot of crazy people. Please come and get me out; I don't belong here."

Mother, Art, and I went as soon as we could to the hospital to visit him. It was several months more before Mother was able to have Errol transferred to another state mental hospital closer to where we lived so that we could visit him often. After months of treatment, his condition improved, and Mother was able to take him home. We don't know what caused Errol's mental illness. It could be that the unhappy experiences of our childhood affected my brothers in a negative way, because my brothers could not forget the pains of our childhood. I am happy to report now that my brother Alan is alive and well; we received a letter from him in 1997, twenty-five years after he had been with us in Los Angeles. He lives in Norway and has a family of his own. Errol, I'm sad to report, has disappeared. We do not know where he is or if he is still alive.

For the first thirty years of my life, I was also in a cold, dark place. I was blaming everyone who had ever hurt me for putting me there. The hurt was great. I blamed my mother, my stepfather, my husband, and everything that was upsetting to me in life. I started to blame Art for some of the deep unhappiness I was experiencing within myself. I felt that I could not be the kind of wife he expected me to be. I was about to give up on life myself, but our three children, whom I loved deeply, made the difference in my will to live.

The thought that our children might have to go through some of the sufferings that I had gone through made me want to be around to protect them, to embrace them with kisses and hugs, and to be always there for them. I wanted them to know that they were loved, that they were not alone in the world, and that somebody cared. Although I loved Art, I felt that he did not really love me and that he would be better off without me, because I was not making him happy, anyway. But after Jesus came into my life, He gradually led me out of that dark place I had almost locked myself into.

Now, in retrospect, I can clearly see that it is not what happens to us in the past that causes unhappiness. No! It is because we allow our negative experiences to control our lives by hanging on to all those deep hurts of the past. Jesus said that we must forgive or we will not be forgiven: *"If you forgive others their transgressions, your heavenly Farther will forgive you, but if you do not forgive others, neither will your Father forgive your transgressions"* (Matthew 6:15).

Jesus knew what He was speaking about. It is true! For, as long as we cling to unhappy memories, we will continue to feel the pain of each past negative experience. Consequently, I listen now to Jesus and try always to follow His instructions. Therefore, I have forgiven everyone in my entire life that has caused me pain. And I pray, daily, that everyone will forgive me for any suffering or unhappiness that I have caused them.

Up to this point in my life, I have not accomplished anything that the world would consider great; yet, God knows how difficult the road has been for me on life's journey thus far. Without Jesus at my side, I would have given up long ago. However, whenever I start to feel sorry for myself, I turn to Jesus for comfort. I know that He is calling me into wholeness and into God's perfection. He wants each of us to give all that we have to life, so that we can enjoy all that life has to give. I have a very long way to go before I reach the perfection to which we are all called—and I may never achieve that noble goal while I'm on this earth. Nevertheless, when the time comes for me to leave this world, I want to be able to say, "I have lived my life on earth to the fullest." That's all God expects from any of us. He would like to bring out the best in us. He is not asking for the impossible.

God knows that life is difficult and that we are weak. That's why He sent us an example to follow. Jesus is our example, and He is the light that God sent into the world, so that we may clearly see the way back to Him. Jesus said: *"Whoever believes in me will do the works that I do, and will do greater ones than these because I am going to the Father. And whatever you ask in my name, I will do, so that the Father will be glorified in the Son"* (John 14:12–13).Jesus never would have said this if He did not know that our potential is unlimited through God the Father. Consequently, we must learn from Jesus to forgive and to love unconditionally.

Love is the precious key that unlocks the door to the joys of life. Yes! Love is the answer. But we can never truly love, unless we first learn to forgive. It is very difficult to completely forgive those who have hurt us. Yet, nothing is impossible with God. As we open our hearts to Jesus, He will teach us and will remove from us all that is not of Him and will fill our hearts instead with His forgiveness and the joy of God's love.

God gave to each of us our own unique gift, which He wants us to share with each other. That's His way of bringing us together as one family in Him; God is calling each of us to love. There are no exceptions. Jesus is the perfect example of love. Everything He did was an example of God's love. Jesus would not have done all that He did if He did not love us. Jesus could have said, "No way! Father, my brothers and sisters are not worth the trouble." Jesus had every reason in the world to change His mind; our Heavenly Father would still have loved Him, but if Jesus had done that, we would never have known what genuine love is. We are reminded by Saint John, in God's Holy Book: *"Whoever is without love does not know God, for God is love"* (1 John 4:8)!

I know that's true, because when I came to know God, I experienced within myself the joy of His transforming love. I want to share with you now a poem in which I expressed my feelings of love. I shared it with my friends and family in the form of a Christmas card in 1983. This poem is entitled, "Love is the Answer."

Love is the Answer

Now the answer is clear.
You can feel it in the air.
It's all around to see, and it's a part of me.
So why did I not know the answer before?
I'll tell you why, my friend.
Without a question, there is no answer
But every questing soul will be enlightened at the end.
And now that night has passed, I can see at last.
So now I'm free, completely free
And the entire world can see
This beautiful substance of which I'm a part
Can be found in everyone's heart
It cannot be purchased, or priced as gold
Yet, it is the seed of man's immortal soul.
Yes, the answer is love. You can feel it in the air.
It's all around to see, and it's the most important part of you and me.
So, let's spread the answer. Then the world will come to know
Love is the answer. And peace is at love's door.

When we learn to approach life with a loving attitude, living becomes an adventure, problems become challenges, hurt feelings are short-lived, and human understanding becomes a genuine pursuit. After God revealed to me that my special gift is communication, I did not know what I should do with it. We had decided in Renew that the gifts of the Holy Spirit were to be shared with the whole community. I spent days wondering how I could share my gift of communication with others. One morning, while walking home after attending Mass, I asked God to tell me how to use my special gift. When I stopped praying, a song that we sometimes sing at church popped into my head. Here are some of the words of that song:

You've got to give all you've got, if you want to get to Heaven
Trust in who I am, for I've come to set you free.
Your days are just a few,
But there's much you can accomplish
So, sell what you've got; give the money to the poor
And come on—yes, come on—come follow me.

I pushed that song from my mind and continued to pray, asking God to please tell me how to use my special gift. Again that song came into my mind. I pushed it away again and continued talking to the Lord. As before, the same words came back into my mind as I continued my walk. I then asked the Lord: "What are you trying to tell me through the words of that song?" My thoughts then focused on these words: *"Sell what you've got and give the money to the poor." Nothing I owned then, or now,* is of any great material value. Therefore, I knew that the Lord was not speaking to me about material things. What I *do* have of real value are my philosophy in life, my belief system, and my faith and trust in God.

Hence, the decision was made to share my feelings about God and life by putting my thoughts into a book. After that decision was made, I had no idea how it would be accomplished. I was working outside the home, I could not type, and my poor spelling ability at times infuriates me. Nonetheless, with all that facing me, I was not discouraged. Jesus was calling me to follow Him, and, since He is my oldest brother and master, I obey. My first thought was to put my poems together in a book, so that I would be able to share them with others. When I started to put the poems together, I decided to write an explanation for each poem to make the book more interesting. The idea developed for this book because of my openness and complete surrender to the Lord's will.

Through the years, I had been scribbling my thoughts out on paper as they came to me. I knew that I would have to write everything out neatly, so that it would be legible for someone else to type. The more I thought about having to write everything out by hand, the more I wished that I could type. My son Dennis was sitting with me at breakfast one morning, and we were discussing my impending book.

I said to Dennis, "Oh, how I wish that I could type!"

He responded, "So, why don't you learn how to type?" He also said, "What you really need is a typewriter with a built-in dictionary."

My eyes popped opened, as I repeated, "A typewriter with a dictionary? Is there such a thing?"

Dennis answered that there was. He had seen one advertised in the newspaper on sale and thought about me when he read the advertisement. (Everyone in our family is aware of my poor spelling skills.) I said to Dennis, "That's wonderful! We must get one."

Art came into the kitchen to join the discussion. He said, "But we already have a typewriter."

"Sure we have a typewriter," I responded. "Its twenty-five years old, and I have tried to learn to type on it, but it's difficult to learn to type on a typewriter that half of the time does not work." Dennis backed me up. The very next Saturday, Dennis, Art, and I went out in search of a typewriter. We went to every store in the neighborhood that sold typewriters, checking each one out.

I did not really know what I was looking for in a typewriter; all I knew was I wanted one with a dictionary. Finally, we got to the store that had advertised the typewriter with the built-in dictionary. Dennis checked out all the typewriters in that store, typing a little on each one, while I just watched.

Then Dennis said, "Here, Mom, this is the one."

My eyes popped open again, as I said, "Let me try it." I tried it and told Art, "This is the typewriter I want, this one has a built in dictionary"

Art said, "Forget it! You don't need such an expensive typewriter to learn to type on." However, with Dennis on my side, we convinced Art. He paid for the typewriter, and we brought it home.

It took me three weeks just to figure out how to operate all the gadgets. I am not yet proficient as a typist, but I am better now than when we first brought that new typewriter home. I will be better still by the time I'm through with this book. The built-in dictionary was a definite aid to me. The typewriter would beep whenever I misspelled a word, so that I could look up the correct spelling. Actually, the built-in dictionary helped me to gain confidence in my spelling ability. Before, I was always checking the dictionary to correct my spelling, even the words that I could spell, so I spent a lot of time with the dictionary. However, while using that typewriter, I would check my spelling only when the typewriter beeped at me.

I love to walk early in the morning. It's a time when I open myself to God as He speaks to me though the beauty of nature. On my walk to church one morning, as I communicated with God, I also observed people on the street. I thought how different we all were; some people walked much slower than I, while others walked much faster, and some zoomed by me in a run that left only the wind in my face. I remembered then something I had read that a psychiatrist had said about human behavior. I can't recall his name, but I recall that he said: "Human personalities come in two categories: some of us are like turtles, while others are like racehorses."

He also said, "You cannot make a turtle move at the speed of a racehorse, nor slow down a racehorse to the pace of a turtle."

I'm like a turtle, but I know the direction in which I'm heading. I'm aware that someone with better typing and spelling skills could write a book much faster than my limited ability allows. In spite of that fact, moving at my own pace, I will eventually get where God is leading me. In God's eyes, the racehorse and the turtle are both perfect, because they are exactly as He created them to be—and in His Kingdom there is a place for each.

In 1 Corinthians 12:12–20, Saint Paul also reminds us of our differences, when he makes a comparison to the unique parts of the body. Saint Paul points out to us that each person, in the Body of Christ, has his or her own special place and is an important part of His Body here on this earth.

A Racehorse I'm Not!

I'm like a turtle!
So I don't move, or learn, as fast as others
And though my burden at times seems heavy
I know who I am, and I am happy to carry my load.
There are advantages to being a turtle
For when night comes, like the turtle that I am,
I take refuge within myself
Knowing that within the shell of my soul God dwells.

Here are some old pictures of me, my mother, and brothers, Alan and Errol. You can see from the pictures that I was a very unhappy child. I have never seen a picture of myself as a child with a smile on my face. As an adult, I did learn to smile as life got better for me.

Madelene and Alan, at ages five and six

Madelene, age twelve, and Mother

Errol, at age five, with Madelene, age eleven

At age nine and eight, Alan and Madelene

Madelene at age sixteen, the year that Mother and Alan left her in Trinidad to live with strangers

Picture a smiling Madelene, in the arms of her beloved husband, Art. Also in picture, is Errol, at the age of sixteen.

I do hope that these pictures included in this book will help you, the reader, to better understand all that I have related about my life, in my childhood and as an adult.

5

A Special Message

But whoever keeps His word,
The love of God is truly perfected in him.
This is the way that we may know that we are in union with Him.

—*1 John 2:5*

We are one in God, and we are all His children. It matters not, where we are or who or what we are. God loves us as we are. That does not mean, however, that we should not grow in understanding of our own imperfections and work diligently to change those things about ourselves that we know are not of God. Change is necessary for growth. God wants us to grow and unfold, so that we can become all that He intended us to be. That's what Jesus is speaking about when He says: *"So be perfect just as your Father in heaven is perfect." (Matthew 5:48)*

Jesus never meant to give us the impression that our heavenly Father would not love us unless we are perfect. God is calling us into His perfection because He wants us to have life and to live it to the fullest. Living life to the fullest means being open to God at all times and allowing Him to teach and renew us. When we reach a point in life when we believe that we know everything we need to know about God or anything else, we close ourselves off from God and stifle our learning process.

To reach God's perfection (as I perceive Jesus' teachings) we must continually grow in the light of love. There is no other way to reach the perfection of which Jesus speaks. You are probably asking yourself, *"If God loves us just the way we are, why strive for perfection?"* It is true—God does love us just the way we are. But we will never completely comprehend nor experience the fullness of God's love until we mature in understanding of our own sinfulness and our need of repentance and forgiveness. Jesus tells us:

"Amen, amen, I say to you, no one can see the kingdom of God without being born from above." (John 3:3) Absolutely! That is the only way anyone can enter or see the Kingdom of God.

"To be born from above," as I understand it, means to enter into the light of Christ without reservations and to follow His teachings at all times, even when it is not popular for us to do so. Therefore, the only way that we can be truly "born again" is to completely surrender our lives to Jesus. We will then mature in our faith and come to realize that Jesus is the only person with the key to His Father's Kingdom. Jesus has the key, because He is perfect. Jesus also has all the answers. He will teach us all that we need to know to become perfect. In God's Kingdom there is no imperfection. When we are the best that we can be, within our own limitations, then we are perfect in God's eyes. The "perfection" that we are called into is the quality, or state, of being open to God and following His instruction to love and forgive at all times, as He loves and forgives us.

After we surrender ourselves completely—mind, soul, and body—then, and only then, will we be transformed into the living Christ. Some of you are thinking now, *"I want to surrender, and I have tried, but nothing is different in my life."* It may be that you are curious about Jesus because of all the wonderful things you have heard about Him. That is not going to do it, my friend. We have to be more than just curious. We must become dead serious about wanting Jesus in our lives. We must make the decision to give up everything to follow Him. That is the only way anyone can be "born again"—in other words, to be renewed, or transformed, we must be totally and completely united with Him.

If you are now ready to make the commitment to follow Jesus, I will show you how to surrender. Go to a quiet place. Sit with your eyes closed. Now, visualize that you are standing beneath Jesus as He hangs on the cross. Look up into His face. See His eyes looking down on you. Tell Him that you are sorry for not trusting Him thoroughly, and tell him that you want to die on the cross with Him to your self-centeredness and of everything else that is not like Him so that you may be resurrected with Him into God's transforming light. Now, in your mind's eye, see yourself stepping out of your own body to be with Jesus on the cross. As you are lifted up to the cross, you will merge with Him into God's transforming light.

I had an elevating experience like this many years ago; it happened while I was in prayer, during an extremely difficult period in my life. It was a beautiful and rewarding experience. This is what I saw in my mind's eye while in prayer:

I saw myself standing beneath the cross of Jesus. I was so sad to see Him all bloody and hanging there. I cried and said: "Lord, I'm so sorry for all the wrong things that I continue to do each day in my life. Please help me to be like you in every way. I want to die to my old self and to be born anew with you."

With that thought, I saw myself hanging on a cross that was on the right side of Jesus'. I looked at myself and then back to Jesus, but He was not on His cross. Instead, I saw Him in a stream of light that was far away from the crosses and above the earth. As I looked in the direction of the light in which He was standing, He motioned for me to come to Him. Instantly, I was also in the light, standing next to Him. At that moment the vision ended, and I was again by myself, but still in prayer. I came out of meditation that day understanding that we must all die to self so that we may also be raised into the resurrected light of Christ.

Having a desire to die on the cross with Jesus is a sign of total surrender, an emptying of oneself, and a step into His Light. If our hearts are sincere and our minds are set on following Jesus, He will be with us every step of the way. Yet, each of us must continue the journey on our own path, and, as we travel with Him, His resurrected light will eventually purify us, so that we may grow into God's perfection. We must, however, trust God. Then He will send His Holy Spirit to teach us, to work with us and through us. On our own human power, there is nothing we can do that will lead us to God. Until we fully understand that concept, life will continue to be an endless struggle in the darkness of our own minds.

The things Jesus is asking us to give up are those which cause destruction in the world: greed, pride, anger, lust, resentment, envy, jealousy, selfishness, self-pity, hurt feelings, and self-righteousness. Jesus is asking us to die to those imperfections, because they are detrimental to our spiritual growth.

Jesus tells us in His Holy Words, through Scriptures, I am the Way, the Truth, and the Life. He also says, No one comes to the Father except through me, and know the truth and it will make you free.

The truth, as I see it, is this: as long as we continue to hold on to our own insecurities, the light of Christ cannot penetrate us. If we want His light to renew us, we must love and forgive. That is the only way that others will see Christ in us. It is very difficult to readily forgive and to forget. But we must, if we want to experience God's unconditional love and grow in His perfection.

When we don't know what we want out of life, we become confused and unhappy. We sometimes find ourselves going in a direction that can get us into a whole lot of trouble. That is not the way God meant it to be. God wants us to have everything in life that will make us happy: peace, joy, and inner contentment. Love and forgiveness of ourselves and others fills us with

God's peace and brings real joy into our lives, along with a spirit of deep contentment.

Christ is the pure light of love that God sent into the world to save us from our own self-destruction. God heard us, His lost children crying for help because we did not know in what direction to go to get out of the darkness of our own sin. God's love is so great that He sent out of Himself the purest of all lights to show us the way back into His beautiful garden of bliss. When we follow Jesus, He will crack the shells of our souls, and His nourishing light will draw forth the substance from the seeds of love that are within us. Then, with the help of God's Holy Spirit, love will take root in our lives and eventually mature to bear fruit in us.

Yes, God wants us to come back to Him, where we will be safe in His nourishing garden. As we read His words, He will instruct us. His words are in the Sacred Scriptures. The Bible is the greatest book that was ever written. That is why it is referred to as Holy. It is whole and complete. Everything we need to know about life and His instructions on the best way to live it is in the Bible. God Himself speaks to us through the pages of His Holy Book. If you do not own a Bible, please get one. We cannot follow Jesus without knowing what He wants us to do. His words are in the Bible, and, as we familiarize ourselves with His teachings, they become a part of us. So, whenever He wants to give us special instructions, He will use those written words to guide us. There is a special verse in the Bible that I would like to share with you now. This verse confirms exactly how I felt about life and all that was happening to me at that time. I begged from the depths of my heart for God to rescue me. He heard my desperate cry and said: "Fear not!"

"...I called upon your name, O Lord, from deep within the well, and you heard me! You listened to my pleading; you heard my weeping! Yes, you came at my despairing cry and told me not to fear."

— *Lamentations.3:55–57:*

Yes! God heard my desperate cry and sent His loving Son, my big brother and Savior. Jesus helped me out of a dark pit, which I could never have gotten out of on my own. Jesus extended His caring hand. I took hold of it and walked right into His light. Jesus is ready to do the same for you. All you have to do is ask Him. Jesus, however, will never force Himself upon anyone. He is kind, gentle, and loving; He is also truly wise. In His wisdom, He knows that unless we are ready to give up everything to follow Him, and that includes our old selves and our old way of thinking, we will be unprepared and unwilling to enter into His light. The perfection that God is calling us to is within everyone's reach. God's seed is in each of us. Of course, we must continuously nurture the seed and unfold in the light of Christ to bear fruit to God's perfection.

If we are called to gardening, for instance, we should not be resentful of the person who is called to be a brain surgeon. Instead, we should set our hearts on becoming the very best gardener that's within us to be. We should give thanks to God for allowing us to plant His beauty in the world for others to enjoy, as we cultivate the wasteland that we see all around us. By so doing, God's perfection will shine through. Then, the best gardener that is within us will come forth. That is how God is calling each of us into His perfection. Yes, in all areas of life, we must love, give of ourselves, and be thankful always for the opportunity to do our part in making our world a better place to live.

Whatever we are called to do, we must do it to the best of our ability in order to achieve inner contentment. There is gratification in knowing that we have done our best. As we do our best, we unfold into the perfection to which we are called. It matters not what God is calling us to be. Everyone has a place in Him. Until we find our places, we will not know Him.

Jesus tells us, *I am in the Father and the Father is in me, and I am in you.* Absolutely! We are all in God and God is in each of us. We are the living body of Christ. He needs us to do His work here on earth, and we need Him to show us how. He is the head and the brains. Without Him, the body (God's people) would be lifeless. So, let's ask for His help. If we want to get to heaven, we must ask Jesus. He will show us how to get there. However, we must be willing to do as He tells us without complaining. For it is far better to be a toenail on the foot of God than to be the head on a serpent. Let us be joyous in all that we do and give glory and praise to God for allowing us to do it!

The human race is the flowering part of God's family tree. God has an immensely large variety of trees in His family. The unique tree that each of us represents must bear fruit or it will dry up. Jesus gave us that message when He cursed the fig tree for not bearing fruit (Matthew 21:18–19). God's seed has produced many different kinds of nourishing fruit in the world (figuratively speaking) but we may never know which fruit God wants us to bring forth, unless we open our hearts to Him.

To find out which of God's fruit we are to bear, we must first cultivate the soil so that the seed within us can grow and unfold to its full potential. It really does not matter what kind of fruit we are destined to bear, as long as we bring it to its fullness. It might be a peach, a cherry, a plum, an orange, or a lemon, just to name a few. (I will have more to share about being a lemon in chapter 14.) Whatever the fruit may be, it will be perfect in God's eyes, for the seed within us is God's—and it will be fully developed. When we fail to become all that we were predestined to be, we are also stifling God's full expression through us, and that, as I perceive it, is a sin.

After we surrender ourselves completely to Jesus, the Holy Spirit of God is given permission to instruct and inspire us. He comes and makes His home in us. Our bodies become holy temples, in which God's Spirit dwells. Then, in the light of the living Christ, we are sustained, nourished, and will mature into everything that we are called to be. Success or failure is only the result of how well we handle the challenges that life presents to us.

I Am a Flower!

I am a flower; that is plain to see.
For I have not yet reached my full capacity
My petals are soft and tender, too;
They absorb the moisture from the dew.
But with God's help, I will survive
As His nourishment flows from deep inside;
Thus, eventually, I know the world will see
The purpose of my bloom is to bring forth
The seed of God's love that's within me!

The gift of life is from God and to God it shall return! The following "God Had a Dream" is my own interpretation of creation. (Please read the book of Genesis for the Biblical version.)

God had a dream in which He saw a beautiful garden. Out of that dream, the earth was formed. God filled His garden with His thoughts, and they were all beautiful. He envisioned the tiniest living creature within the earth, and the most magnificent creatures He placed upon the earth and in the sky above. God looked upon His creation and was pleased. God saw the wonderful world that He had created. God said then: "I will now create special creatures that will be above all others. [These unique creatures would be man and woman.] They will be like me [please see Genesis 1:27] and, therefore, will be different from all the other creatures, because they will be my children and I will be their Father. In them I will place my seed, and that seed will be the seed of life, and I will teach them how to live and be happy, through guidance of My Holy Spirit. My children will know that I love them, because I will give them my own power to be creative. My children will love me," God thought, "and they will want to get to know me as I know them. But I will never interfere in their lives, for they will be given total freedom to use their own creative ability to learn all they should learn and to be all that they can be."

That's the way it was. God created the earth so that we could live with

Him in harmony and peace in His beautiful garden of bliss, with everything we need to grow and learn as His children. Years passed, and God observed us as we developed. He noticed that some of His children were doing just fine, keeping in touch with Him and growing in His light. But some, He noticed, were having a lot of trouble with the freedom that He had given them.

God then thought: *I must help my children. I will not take away their freedom, but I will make some suggestions that I know will help them.*

Because God does love us, He gave us rules to help us stay out of trouble. Those rules are the Ten Commandments. Some of God's children, however, continued to do their own thing, disregarding the rules that Our Loving Father had carefully put together for our protection. Consequently, by ignoring those rules, we drifted out of God's nourishing garden and into a dangerous place in which God's light wasn't there to protect us. We were moving deeper and farther into a land of darkness, until we were so far away from God's protection that we could no longer hear His loving voice. The only voice that God's lost children could hear was the voice of darkness. And that voice lied to us and led us farther away from God and deeper into darkness.

God saw the spirit of death deceiving His lost children, and He knew that it had become impossible for us to find our way back into His beautiful garden. So He thought of a good plan by which He could save us, without taking away our freedom. God knew that He must send a light into the darkness. Thus, God sent out from Himself the purest of all lights, like no other light the world had ever seen. And that light continues to shine to this day for everyone on earth to follow.

Jesus is that pure light of God, the only light that can penetrate the darkness of our souls, and He is always available to those who call upon Him for help. Yet, with our human eyes, we don't see Him. To see Jesus, we must open our hearts, for the heart is the dwelling place of God.

In Hebrew, it is said; the word for "heart" means not only the seat of the emotions, but the entire inner being! This includes the intellect, memory, imagination, feelings, and the will, which is the source of one's thoughts, words, and actions. Yes, indeed, the whole person. That's how we must look for Jesus. Then we will find Him—when we have completely surrendered ourselves, our entire beings, to Him.

We need to renew our minds, to learn who Christ is, and to take on a fresh way of thinking. We need to dream of new things and new places. We need to use the imagination that God gave us to be creative. We need to be as Christ is, to change our lives and the world around us. Yes, God had a dream, and it was a beautiful dream.

We, too, as His faithful children can become a living part of that dream. We can—and should—claim our inheritance as obedient children of God. In every moment of each day, we should live in the presence of God and in the company of Jesus. We should dream of becoming like Jesus: to feel as He feels, to see as He sees, to understand as He understands, to love as He loves, and to know God as He knows God. We should also dream of bringing forth from within us the seed of God's love, so that we might bear fruit to that love. The only fruit that is everlasting and life-giving is the fruit of God's love. When everyone learns to love as God Himself loves us, then, we will be able to give birth to Jesus in this world. Like Mary, our Blessed Mother, we too will say yes to God: *"Let it be done to me according to your word."* (Luke 1:38)

My wish is that everyone on earth will not only taste the sweetness of God's love in their lives, but will also chew, swallow, and digest its nourishment.

I will share with you now a song that I wrote a long time ago. At that time in my life, I was questioning my own ability to grow. I am not a musician, so I cannot include the musical notes. The melody is in my head

Have I Set My Goals Too High?

Have I set my goals too high?
Or is life a foolish dream?
Am I just a senseless child?
Reaching for a star
Thinking it's not too far?
Have I set my goals too high?
Wondering if I should live or die?
I know to live I must keep trying
To make my life worthwhile
But have I set my goals too high?
Should I awaken from this dream?
Ending my belief that life
Is more than what it seems?
Have I set my goals too high?
Should I stop myself from growing?
And wanting to unfold,
Hoping that someday I may reach my goal?
Who can answer me? "To be or not to be"
My true self is my quest to peace and happiness
If I have set my goals too high,
Life for me would fade away.
I would just cease to be,
But my soul would then be free,
To find its rightful place, in the sky!

I have given a lot of thought to that question, and the answer is a definite no! I have not set my goals too high. God is calling me, and everyone on this earth, into His perfection, in all aspects of our lives, to bring out from within us the very best of ourselves: the best employee, wife, husband, mother, father, neighbor, and Christian. Again, that is the kind of perfection Jesus is speaking to us about. When we know in our hearts that we have done everything in our power to bring out the best of ourselves, we become outgoing and positive individuals. We may not always be able to please everyone in our lives, and even when we know we have done our very best some individuals may still be unhappy with our performance. But God will know. He will be pleased, and we will be rewarded for our efforts.

Go for the Gold

The road may be narrow
And the mountain be high
But the trip to the top is a journey worthwhile;
So hang on to your smile and be always aware
There's someone at your side with helping hands to share.
Never forget your teammates are near;
Just help them along and let them know that you care
So when you get to the top, you'll be there with friends
Then you'll be awarded the gold where the rainbow ends.

So let's love one another and extend helping hands to each other—as we continue our own journeys along the way, in the light of Jesus Christ, our loving brother and Savior. "Go for the Gold" was published in Gottschalks' magazine, The Big "G" Retailer, in September 1997. The manager of Gottschalks Department Store in Palm Springs, Mr. Skip King, liked the poem when I recited it at an employee's breakfast meeting. After the meeting, he asked me for a copy and told me that he was going to send it to corporate, because he felt that it reflected the "Gottschalks Culture" and could be a good reminder and inspiration for all. He did send it, and Gottschalks published it.

6

Dreams and Experiences with God

I will instruct you and show you
The way that you should walk
Give you counsel, and watch over you.

—Psalms 32:8

Experts say that we dream every night, and I am sure that we do. Most of us, however, just do not remember our dreams. I am no exception. Yet, I have had some dreams throughout my life that did not seem like dreams. I remember every detail of those dreams as if they were real experiences.

Shortly after Jesus appeared to me in 1963, I frequently dreamt about Egypt. It seemed to be all I dreamt about. One night I dreamt that I was in Egypt and found myself in a place that looked like a museum. There were ancient relics and dinosaur skeletons in a huge room. When I entered that room, a group of people joined me. We were all dressed exactly alike, wearing white long-sleeved, floor-length robes. It seemed as if we were on a guided tour, because we were being led by someone through the huge room. We continued to follow him until we came to a door. We all stopped in front of that door. Our guide unlocked the door, turned the knob, opened the door, and then motioned to us with his right hand to follow him.

We entered into a smaller room. I could see everything in that room. The room was white and very clean. In the center of the room was a table that looked like a surgical table, one that you would find in an operation room of a modern-day hospital. The leader instructed us, by motioning with his hand, to gather around the table. As we came near the table, I noticed that there was a cutting board on the table. The cutting board had a tiny knife on it. Our instructor reached over his head and brought a hanging light closer to the cutting board.

As he refocused the light, he spoke for the first time and said: "There is an old Egyptian proverb that says…" As he said that, he reached into his pocket and took out something that looked like a green pea. He held the pea to the light for all to see and, continuing to speak, he said, "The seed bore fruit and the fruit gives us life." He then put the pea on the cutting board, holding it with his left hand between his thumb and forefinger, and with his right hand he took the tiny knife, cut the pea in half, and opened it up. In the center of that pea there was a tiny leg of lamb. The dream ended.

I got out of bed and made breakfast for my family. I could not get the dream out of my head. It continued to haunt me throughout the day. I kept thinking about that proverb, "The seed bore fruit and the fruit gives us life." I kept asking myself, "What does it mean?" Later that day, I went to a library in our neighborhood to see if I could find a proverb similar to that one, Egyptian or otherwise. In the library I could not find any proverb exactly like that one. I read everything the library had on proverbs. I found many proverbs about seeds and fruit, but I could find nothing exactly like the one in my dream.

The next day I went to another library, out of our neighborhood, and read everything that library had on proverbs. However, I still could not find a proverb like the one in my dream. That proverb stayed constantly in my mind throughout the week. I could not stop thinking about it. Even in church the following Sunday, I was still thinking about that proverb. The priest held up the Host, (the Eucharistic bread) and said, "This is the Lamb of God, who takes away the sins of the world. Happy are those who are called to His supper." As I repeated that prayer, a light flashed in my head, and the full meaning of the proverb that had been haunting me all week was made clear. I was so filled with joy that tears flowed down my cheeks. I realized then that the Lord Himself was instructing me. The pea in the dream represented the seed that gives life to everything. That "seed" is God. The leg of lamb represents Jesus. The lamb was brought forth out of God's seed, so that we might take Him into our bodies, souls, and minds, as the eternal food of life that nourishes and sustains us. Read John 6:53–59.

Another time, I dreamt I was out in space. I had no body and floated freely with the stars, as if I were on my way to heaven. I looked back at the earth and could see it moving as it rotated. Then I heard a voice. I saw no one. The voice, which was very deep, said to me, "God is the invisible electromagnetic force that keeps the earth moving on its course." With that, I awoke.

The memory of that dream was so vivid, I felt as though I had really been out in space. For the next few days, all that I had experienced in that dream stayed with me, as I wondered what it meant. I continued to recall that dream, and the words the voice had spoken remained in my mind through the years to become a part of my thinking. It was then I started looking for God everywhere and finding Him in everything!

Because of those dreams, the poem "God Is Seeded in Man's Soul" came to me. Shortly after I had that dream, I read an article in a woman's magazine entitled: "God is Dead." That article so infuriated me that I wanted to write something in response to it. Therefore, I wrote this poem.

God Is Seeded in Man's Soul

Although the sky is dark at night
God can be seen in each twinkling light,
And as the birds wing through the air
They sing his melody sweet and clear.
God is in the ocean, the rain, and the warm sunshine
He's in everything that preserves mankind.
All natural marvels one sees and hears
Are proof that He is everywhere!
He's in the wind, when the day is bright
And yet He's in the stillness of the night
There are those who say: "God does not exist"
Although His presence can be seen in the midst
Of the forest greenery, a mountain's wall
And in the loveliness of a waterfall!
God is in every miraculous living thing
He is the beauty of the winter, and He is the life of spring
He's the current that makes a river flow;
He's the ingredient that enables man to grow.
Yes! God is the nucleus and accretions of growth.
His seed impregnated the earth
Thus the "seed bore fruit and the fruit gives us life."
Nonetheless, man needs strong roots to survive,
So when we draw our nourishment from deep below
We gain our natural strength to grow,
And if mankind continues to blossom without fading away
We will all bear fruit to God's unconditional love some day.
And when humanity has reached its maturity
Only then will we see
The perfect sons and daughters God intended us all to be.
Hence, the story of Christ will forever be told
For He is God's only perfect Son, the one who gives nourishment to the world;
Yes, indeed, Jesus is the key

That unlocked the door for me, to God's real mystery.
Now I can see humanity's true capacity.
For we are all a part of God's life-giving seed,
And we are all connected to the same nourishing roots
That has nourished some men into immortals.
Therefore, God is "the invisible electromagnetic force
That keeps the earth moving on its course."
And so is He the power within that keeps man inevitably journeying.
Yes! God is the illimitable essence of life
And He is the brain of the universe!
So, children of this world
Come take this trip with me;
Travel within; then you, too, will surely see
That which man seeks is hidden inside.
When we have all learned that truth
Humankind will have arrived
Then! The "seed" of love, wisdom and immortality
Will take root in our lives
To bring forth its fruits of fulfillment!

Another dream remains vivid in my mind to this day. That dream was about a beautiful place. While I was dreaming, I thought, "This must be heaven! It feels so wonderful being here." Also, in this dream I had no body, and I just floated with the clouds over the beautiful meadows, valleys, rivers, and lakes. I remember thinking, *"I do not want to ever leave this place."* Consequently, on awakening I was sad that the dream had ended. I went into the bathroom with my eyes closed and kept wishing that when I got back to bed the dream would continue. It was the middle of the night, so I got back into bed remembering the dream. As I fell asleep, I got my wish. I went back to that beautiful place in the same dream. Everything in that dream was in magnificent color. The sky was bright blue, the grass and trees were deep green, the flowers were yellow and orange, the river was crystal clear, and the lake reflected the blue of the sky. When I awoke the next morning, I felt as though I had indeed been to heaven. I shared that experience with everyone in my family. As I told them about it, I said, "Oh, how I wish I could paint. If only I knew how, I would paint a picture of that beautiful place, so that everyone could see it."

Years later, our daughter Noelle was taking art lessons. She was learning to paint with oils, and. I thought she was doing very well. I bought a canvas and asked her to paint a picture for me to hang over our bed. She said she that would as soon as she became more proficient. Months passed. Noelle continued to take art lessons, but she still would not touch my canvas. I became a little annoyed with Noelle for ignoring my request. While we were discussing the matter, we had a disagreement about her artistic ability. I thought Noelle had great possibilities as an artist. However, she disagreed with me and said, "I don't know how to paint. I'm not an artist, and I don't want to ruin another canvas!" Well! With that firm statement from Noelle I knew that if I wanted a picture painted on my canvas, I would have to do it myself.

I told everyone in my family what I had decided to do. They laughed at me. I really could not blame them for laughing. Up to that point in time, I had shown no artistic ability, and, to this day, I still do not have any real ability as an artist. In spite of that, with brush in hand, I began to paint on my canvas. I had no idea what I was going to paint. I knew only that I was going to try to paint something to hang over our bed. We had recently redecorated our bedroom, and Art had paneled the wall behind our bed. So I thought if I could just put some color on the canvas that would complement the colors in the bedroom, it would be interesting. But as I began to paint, I suddenly remembered that heavenly place in that beautiful dream, which I had experienced many years before. As I moved the paintbrush over the canvas, I did paint (to the best of my limited ability) that place as I remembered it from my dream. That painting is not a perfect work of art, and my lack of artistic talent is obvious to anyone who knows how to paint. Yet, this fact is evident: having the desire to put on canvas the beautiful place that I had visited in my dream, I made the desire become a reality. I had to do another painting to hang over our bed, however, because the colors in my dream painting were not right for the bedroom. I was excited about my new ability to paint, so I continued to experiment on my own. I have had no art lessons, but I'm sure you will be able to see that as you view my paintings.

This painting represents what I experience in my dream. That heavenly place was more magnificent than I am capable of expressing with a paint brush. Yet, to the best of my (inadequate) ability, through this painting I try to share my experience by recalling everything I remembered about that heavenly place and painting a picture for everyone to see. The white object in the sky is my interpretation of what I felt like in that dream. I did not have a body. I just floated with the clouds over beautiful mountains, meadows, rivers, and lakes. The colors were vibrant blues, greens, yellow, orange and transparent white clouds.

Heaven Is

Heaven is in a sky of blue.
It's a field of flowers and a philosophy, too.
It a scenic trip, a restful cruise
It is the excitement that comes with enjoyable news.
It's the ecstasy of love when it is well shared.
It's the pleasure we get in being with those for whom we care.
Yes, heaven could be the weather, a place, or anything,
For I have found heaven through my own thinking.
Thus, heaven is a state of mind
And happiness is the same you'll find.
And, as hell is the worse agonizing pain,
Heaven is the greatest joy anyone can gain.
Heaven then, is like the essence of spring,
Its fragrance enhances everything.
So, take advantage, enter in.
Then you will know the eternal Being.
And as His presence, is forever near.
Heaven is with Him everywhere!

I wrote the poem "Heaven Is" while experiencing a lot of pain with hemorrhoids. That problem has since been corrected surgically, but on that day I was in so much pain that the only way I could get any relief was to lie on the floor flat on my back with my feet high above my head. It was Thanksgiving, and everyone in our family was at our home for dinner. I had been on my feet all day preparing the meal. I was very uncomfortable and had suffered all through that day. After dinner I excused myself and told everyone that I did not feel well and had to lie down. I left the table, went into my bedroom, closed the door behind me, and started to cry, as I prayed to God to take away the pain.

As I prayed, the pain finally went away, but I continued to talk to God. I said, "Father, why do you let me suffer this way? Please heal me of this painful condition." Then I said, "Well, if you are not going to heal me, I guess I will just have to go see a doctor. Maybe he will help me."

When I stopped praying, I started thinking pleasant thoughts about all the beautiful things I had seen in the world and remembering all the fun we have had as a family on our many camping trips. I began then to thank God for all His blessings. As I thought of these things, the poem "Heaven Is" flowed into my mind.

Years ago, after I had made the decision to go to work to help out financially, I'd had no idea where to look for work or what I was going to do. So, like any good child of God, I turned it over to Him. One day, I was in a beautiful department store just looking around and checking everything out. The thought came to me that this would be a lovely place to work because of the pleasant surroundings. With that thought, I went to the personnel office and left my application with them.

Two weeks later, I was called back for an interview and was offered a job. The job they offered me was in the drapery department, on the third floor. I felt that I would not be happy working in the drapery department, because that department was in a corner with no windows and was too closed in. I thanked them for offering me the job, but said I would be much happier working in a department on the second floor. I named three departments in which I thought I could do the best job. The gentleman who interviewed me said, "Thank you for coming in, Mrs. Balloy. We will call you again when there is an opening in one of those departments." I thanked him and left. I went home thinking I might have made a mistake by not accepting the job he had offered me. I also thought that he might not call me back, because he was probably thinking that I had been too particular.

Three days later, the phone rang. I picked it up and the voice said, "This is Robinsons Department Store calling. We have an opening in a department in which we know you will enjoy working; it's one of the three you requested."

I accepted the job and worked in the fashion jewelry department for over a year. I then moved to the cosmetics department, where I worked for nine years. I really enjoyed working in that department. I made many good friends there who were like an extension of my own family. We had our ups and downs, but we always worked out our disagreements.

After about six years of working in the cosmetic department, I began to get restless. I wondered if I shouldn't be doing something else with my life. At the same time, I was also having female problems. I eventually had to have a hysterectomy to correct the problem. Ten weeks later, I went back to work, but the job had lost its appeal. I no longer enjoyed the experience; on top of that, I was still not feeling well. I had not completely recovered from surgery. So I worked part-time, about five hours a day and I eventually decided to quit altogether.

Art was doing very well in his construction business at that time and could use my assistance with all the paperwork. For ten months I stayed home helping Art and thoroughly enjoying the freedom to do whatever I wanted to do with my life. But my freedom soon ended when the bottom fell out of the economy. Art's construction business hit rock bottom. I was forced to go back to work and was very unhappy about the prospect. I could not decide where to go to find work. The economy was slow, and there were not many jobs available. I prayed, asking God what I should do

I called the manager of the cosmetics department at Robinsons. She told me there were no openings at the time and, because business was very slow, they were not hiring. I began to worry and wished I had not left my former job there. It was obvious that I needed to find work somewhere. Our savings were depleted, and we had to refinance our home to pay off some pressing bills. When you own a business and money is coming in, that's great! But when there is no money coming into the business, the bills must still be paid, or you will lose everything. As I was trying to type a resume, I continued to pray, asking God to help me and to show me where to find work. My mind wandered away from the resume, and instead I typed this poem.

Hasten Darkness in Its Flight

In my mind today I feel discouraged,
Yet, my heart tells me that I should not be.
So, Heavenly Father, please, speak to me
In a language that I can understand.
Help me to see Thy perfect plan
Is safe as always in your hand
If only I could realize
What Thy will is for me.
I think then I could sit and wait
Until I've reached my enlightened state.
But, life goes on, as it must
Even when my time has passed!
So, fill me with Thy perfect light,
Hasten darkness in its flight,
Let the world see me, as I should be
A shining example of Thee!

I left the typewriter, because my heart was saddened with the thought of not being able to find work. Our children were still in school, and our concern was for them. We did not want to sell our home and uproot the children from their schools. I was crying when the phone rang. The lady calling was from Saint Bernardine's religious education department. She called to ask me if I would pick up a film in Los Angeles that day for the Christian Education Department. The film had to be picked up the same day that it was going to be shown and returned the next day. I had volunteered my services to that department to drive to Los Angeles to pick up any material, whenever it was needed. As I drove to LA to pick up the film, I continued to speak to God, telling Him all that was in my heart. When I arrived at the archdiocesan office, the lady at the desk was expecting me, and she had the film ready. I thanked her as she gave it to me and immediately crossed the street to visit the beautiful old church that was directly across from the office.

I went into the church and looked around to find a quiet place where I could be alone with God. On the right side of the church there was an area that was empty. I entered the pew, knelt for a few minutes, sat down, and continued to ask God to answer my prayer. While I was sitting there in prayer, I drifted off into a blissful state, a state of mind in which I felt at peace with myself, knowing somehow that all was well. As I sat there with my mind still and my thoughts quiet, I heard a voice within myself saying, "Go to Robinsons." I was startled. I opened my eyes and thought, "Robinsons? I have already done that and was told they are not hiring now because of the slow economy." Nevertheless, in spite of own negative thinking, I did stop at Robinsons on my way home.

As soon as I entered the cosmetic department, one of my friends came running over to me, with arms wide open. As we embraced, she said to me, "I'm so glad you came in today, Madelene. I have been thinking about you and was planning to call you as soon as I got home tonight to tell you to call Thelma right away—because one of the ladies in Estee Lauder Cosmetics department gave her notice today!"

Thelma was the manager of the cosmetics department. I immediately went over to my friend, Lola, the one who had given her notice that day, to find out why she was leaving Estee Lauder and Robinsons. Lola told me that she and her husband, Ross, had bought a home in Lake Tahoe, Nevada, and had decided that's where they wanted to live and work. Thelma Plough saw me at the Estee Lauder counter speaking with Lola and came over to greet me. She said to me, "Lola gave notice today that she is leaving us, but I'm not sure when the store will replace her, because we are not doing any hiring now." Two weeks later I was back at Robinsons, working in the cosmetic department behind the Estee Lauder counter.

I continued to work at Robinsons in the cosmetic department for three more years. After that time, restlessness began to stir in me again. I felt it was time for a change. So I left my job at Robinsons and went to work at another department store for an increase in salary. But the new job did not ease my restlessness. As a matter of fact, I was very unhappy in that new job. I felt I had made a terrible mistake giving up the security I had with Robinsons and leaving behind all my friends with whom I had worked for so many years. Before I left my job at Robinsons, I had prayed much about it. I felt the Lord was calling me to make a change. Yet, I was uneasy about leaving. So I prayed, asking God to let me know if He really wanted me to leave Robinsons. I felt all the signs were pointing me in that direction.

In spite of that, after I took that new job, everything that could go wrong went wrong. I could not understand what was happening and why the Lord would want me in a place where I was so unhappy. I even got my first traffic ticket during the first week on the new job. Since my "born again" experience, I have become a happy and outgoing person, looking for the good in every situation. But discontentment continued to plague me on that new job. I was confused. But, as always, I turned it over to God. I would talk to Him every morning on my walk to church. I loved to walk. It gave me a good feeling and an opportunity to work out my frustrations first thing in the morning. At that time I was also having trouble with bunions, and, as I walked, they throbbed, which made walking quite uncomfortable. Thus, I talked to God about that, too, and prayed that He would heal them. Instead, they became even more painful.

Needless to say, I had to eventually take time off from my new job to have them surgically removed. While recovering from that surgery, I had to stay off my feet for two months. It was then that the Lord inspired me to formulate all that I had previously written, to make some sense of it. I had been thinking about putting my poems together in a little book ever since the Renew program. But I had never seemed to have enough time to do it. Now, however, having to stay off my feet because of the surgery gave me the perfect opportunity to begin the book. I became aware then that the restlessness that had forced me to change jobs was God's call to me to move out and beyond this mundane world into a new and higher place. Yes, *"All things happen for good to those who love God and are called according to His purpose."* (Romans 8:28).

We can, indeed, be instructed by God in our dreams and throughout the day, as we listen for His voice in the silence of our minds. In His Holy Book, He instructs us to "Be still and know that I am God."

On our wedding anniversary in 1974, when I arrived home from work, beautiful flowers from Art were awaiting me! I wanted to capture the beauty of the colors so that I could enjoy them forever.

This one I did to hang over our bed to replace the dream painting. As you can see, these two works are not perfect works of art. But I was pleased with myself, because I had managed to place on canvas the desire I had in my heart.

"A Cypress Tree at Monterey:" Our family was on a camping trip at Big Sur, California. On a sightseeing trip, we encountered this tree. We were all fascinated by it: a tree growing out of a rock at the ocean. We took a picture of it. After returning home from our trip, I created this painting.

"The Masked Lady:" In a dream about Egypt, I was this woman. I thought at that time that this person represented something about me that needed to be unmasked. I have since discovered that what needed to be revealed was a true evaluation of my hidden self.

7

VISIONS

Jesus went up the mountain
And summoned those whom
He wanted, and they came to him.

—*Mark 3:13*

God speaks to us in many ways: through our restlessness, in our consciences, through others, and in visions and dreams. When we are open to God, we hear His voice and see His face in the innermost depths of our souls.

After recovering from foot surgery, I had to make a decision about going back to work. The thought of going back to work in that store was upsetting to me. Working there was not a pleasant experience. I felt locked in and did not have the freedom to be myself and to serve customers in the manner that I was able to while working at Robinsons. At that new store we were evaluated by how much we sold in an hour. Most of the people that I worked with in the cosmetic department did paperwork and stock work off the clock so that our sales per hour would not be affected. The pressure put on us for high sales per hour is just one of many unhappy memories of my experiences in that store.

One day, in meditation, while still on medical leave after foot surgery, I saw myself on a mountaintop with Jesus. As the vision unfolded, I saw that Art, Noelle, and Dennis were also with us. (At the time of that vision, Noelle and Dennis were still living at home.) My family and I were walking along with Jesus. We stopped walking when we got to a fork at the end of the road. As the vision continued, we were just standing in the middle of that road looking around, as if we could not make a decision as to where we should go next.

Then I noticed that Jesus had gone ahead of us, as if to check out the area. My family and I just stood there, waiting for His instructions. As the vision continued, I saw Jesus standing at the top, near the edge of that mountain. As my attention returned to Jesus, He motioned to me with His hand to come to Him. I ran to Him, putting my right arm around His waist. We stood there with His left arm around my shoulders. He pointed with His right hand in a direction beyond where we were standing. I looked out and over the edge of the mountain into the valley below.

There was a higher mountain ahead of where we were standing. In the narrow valley between the two mountains I could see a very busy city, with tall buildings and heavy traffic moving in both directions. As I looked down on that city between the two mountains, lost in thought, Jesus spoke and said, "Well?" as if waiting for my decision. I looked at Him and said in reply, "No! Lord, I want to stay here with you." After I answered Him, I saw the city below us being washed away as if flooded by a river. I watched with uneasiness, as I wondered what was going on and why Jesus had flooded the city beneath us.

I came out of meditation but remained prayerful, as I asked God to explain to me the meaning of what I had just seen. For days I prayed about that vision, trying to understand what it meant. I felt the need to share that vision with someone, so I called my friend Minica Bond, inviting her to have lunch with me. Minica and I had become instant friends the very first day that we had had lunch together at Robinsons. We worked together in the cosmetic department for about a year before I left to take the new job. Minica was very close to Jesus. I could share everything about myself and what I was experiencing on my journey with Jesus. Over lunch I shared the vision, and asked her what she thought it meant. She said "I don't really know, Madelene, but I do know that water is cleansing." I thanked Minica for her insight, and we parted.

That evening, I went again into prayerful meditation and found myself back on the same mountain with Jesus. We were walking together along the edge of the mountain and talking. As we were deep in conversation I realized I had lost sight of my family. I looked around and said to Jesus, "Lord, what about my family? I can't leave them behind!" Jesus said, "Okay, they can come with us." He then snapped His fingers and a bridge appeared from the side of the mountain on which we were standing. My family was again with us. As I stood at the edge of that mountain with Jesus and my family, looking at the bridge, it moved out from the side of the mountain and attached itself to the mountain that was beyond and in front of us. The bridge was the kind you might find in a wilderness. It was made of rope and woven together as if by hand. The bottom and sides were all made of the same material. It looked like a huge hammock. There was a rope at the top on each side of the bridge. With hands grasping the ropes to balance ourselves, we walked over the bridge and headed to the new mountain. My family was the first to get on the bridge.

As I continued to observe all that was taking place, I noticed that the bridge was now moving away from the high mountain that was just ahead of us. My family was having such a good time on the bridge. We were all laughing and trying to stay on our feet, as we crossed over to the other side of the mountain. The bridge finally stopped moving as it came to the high mountain that had been ahead of us. It attached itself to the lower side of that mountain. Noelle was the first person to get off the bridge. We all followed her.

There were other people in that place, and they all seemed to know Noelle. As they came over to greet her, she was jumping in excitement, as she shouted for all to hear, "I made it! I made it!" It was as if she knew all along where she was going and was so happy to finally get there. While observing all that was happening, my thoughts were, "*This is my vision. How, then, does everyone in this place seem to know Noelle?*" With that thought, I stood there looking around and observing everything. My meditation ended, yet I could not erase from my mind what I had seen in the vision. My thoughts flowed into prayers, throughout the night and the next day, asking God to please reveal to me what that vision meant.

The next evening I went into the quiet of our bedroom to sit in prayer and meditation before dinner. Meditation before dinner was a part of my daily routine for more than twenty years. As I quieted my mind to a state that was at peace with itself, I found myself back in the same place as the day before. The vision continued. I noticed that everyone was dressed alike, wearing long, flowing white robes. I also noticed that the people there were in a state of rest. Some were walking around with books in their hands, reading; others were sitting reading or writing, and others were just quietly meditating.

This place in my vision was very peaceful and quite beautiful. There were unusual trees and flowers. A small waterfall trickled down the mountainside and fell into a natural pool. From the pool there flowed a little stream that appeared to be moving through the whole area. I also noticed some people walking on a path up the side of the mountain, while others continued their individual pursuits. As I observed all that was happening, I also noticed the sky. It was a very unusual color, an orange-yellow. I got the impression that night never fell there and that the color of the sky was a reflection from the mountain directly above.

My meditation ended. I went into the kitchen to prepare dinner. All through the evening, and the next day, I could not forget what I had seen in my vision. I wondered what God was teaching me through all that I had seen. I also wondered if God had allowed me to view a small part of heaven and if it was a special resting place that some souls would go to for a short time after death. But I really did not know what it all meant, and to this day I'm still wondering.

The next evening, as usual, I went again into prayer and meditation. As before, I returned to the same place in my vision; however, this time I focused on my family and noticed they were all gathered around the Blessed Mother. I wondered what her presence meant. My attention drifted to the path on the side of the mountain, where I had seen people walking toward the top the day before. Now Jesus was standing on that path by Himself and motioning to me to come to Him. I ran to Him, as I said, "There you are! I was wondering where you were." With my right arm around His waist, and His left arm around my shoulder, we began walking on the path that seemed to be taking us to the top of the high mountain.

We walked together, just talking. Jesus said He wanted to show me something. As we continued to walk, I answered, "Yes, Lord; show me." After walking for some time, Jesus and I were by ourselves on that part of the mountaintop. Suddenly I stopped, turned around, and noticed that we were a long way from where we had left my family.

"Lord! My family! They are not with us," I cried.

Jesus answered, "Yes, I know, but I want you to come with me now."

I just stood there with tears in my eyes, as I asked again, "But, Lord, what about my family? I don't want to leave them!"

Jesus came up to me, put both His hands on my shoulders, and stood in front of me to comfort me. He said, "Madelene, your family is okay. I left them in the care of My Mother. You don't have to worry about them anymore. Your prayers have been answered. They are in a safe place. No harm will come to them. But I want you now to be with me." We continued our walk together up the path that was taking us higher to the top of that mountain.

Although I had Jesus as my companion, my heart was saddened at the thought of leaving my family behind. I wondered if I would ever see them again. As my thoughts wandered back to my family, I could see them walking around in the place where we had left them. They were so interested in what was going on there they did not seem concerned that I wasn't there with them. I realized then that I could be with my family any time I wanted to be with them. But now Jesus wanted my undivided attention so that He could teach me all I needed to learn about His Heavenly Kingdom. That was a turning point in my life. I understood that there is only so much that we can do for those we love. The rest they must do for themselves.

8

INTRODUCTION TO PETER

Do you know that you are the temple of God?
And that the Spirit of God dwells in you?

—*1 Corinthians 3:16*

In a lecture I once attended at my friend Minica's church, we were told that visions are an extension of dreams. The nun who presented the talk that evening explained to us how God speaks to us through our dreams. I had shared with Minica some of my many interesting dreams, so she knew that I would be interested in this subject. That nun had a degree in psychology. Thus she was invited as a guest speaker to help us get a better understanding of our dreams and how we could learn about ourselves from them. She declared to us, "An active mind will also have visions." My mind must be very active!

My walk with Jesus continued for months through visions. Every time I went into prayer and meditation, I would be with Jesus, and we were covering a lot of ground. One day after we left my family with the Blessed Mother, I was with Jesus on the mountaintop, when suddenly there was someone else with us, as well. As I wondered who he was, Jesus said, "Madelene, this is Peter."

I was so surprised, and I thought to myself, "What is Peter doing on my mountaintop in my vision?"

I came out of meditation, but I could not get the thought of Peter out of my mind. I thought then, "My mind is playing tricks on me! I should probably close my mind to these visions and just force myself to pray during meditation." Yet I could not get Peter out of my mind. I was wondering what it was about Peter that Jesus wanted me to know.

As I came out of my bedroom, Noelle came out of hers at the same time and we bumped into each other in the hallway. She said, "Sorry, Mom."

I looked at her and said, "Noelle, a very strange thing happened in my meditation today."

She continued to walk into the bathroom. I followed her and said, "Jesus introduced me to Peter!"

Noelle said, "So?"

I responded with, "But he was in my meditation, as I walked with Jesus on my mountain!"

Noelle retorted, "So what?"

I answered her, "I just don't understand why he was there."

Noelle replied, "Maybe Jesus wants you to read Peter."

"Maybe you're right!" I said.

I left the bathroom, went immediately to my Bible, and read 1 Peter and 2 Peter.

I was impressed by what Peter was saying through his letters to the people of God. Peter's letters are not complicated. They are written in a language that anyone can understand. His instructions are clear and precise, explaining to the best of his ability all that was happening and all that will happen to God's people, who Jesus Christ is, and His purpose among us. Peter explains in his letters how we should live our lives as children of God if we want to get to Heaven. I hope you take some time to read 1 and 2 Peter.

The next evening during meditation and prayer, I was back on the mountain again with Jesus—and Peter. As we walked together, I asked Jesus, "Why is Peter here with us?"

Jesus answered, "I wanted you to meet Peter, because you are a lot like him." Jesus then turned to Peter and said to him, "Isn't that right, Peter?"

Peter answered with a smile in his voice, as he said, "That's right!"

I came out of meditation wondering how I was like Peter. I'm still wondering! Peter was not an educated man; he was a fisherman. Yet, when Jesus asked his twelve disciples if they were going to leave Him too (some of Jesus' followers had started to leave Him because they did not understand all that Jesus was saying to them), Simon Peter answered and said, *"Master, to whom shall we go?"* (Read John 6:60–69).

I know that Peter was a true disciple of Jesus. He did not always understand everything that Jesus was teaching him, and sometimes Peter would get himself in trouble with Jesus, because he would say things that were not of the Holy Spirit. Nevertheless, his heart was in the right place. It was with Jesus. and Peter knew that Jesus was the Christ, the Son of the Living God. That was the only time that Peter was on my mountain. I have not seen him since.

Through the years since I met Peter, I have given much thought to how I am like him. I am not holy, and I'm certainly not a saint! However, like Peter, I am not particularly bright and do not always understand all that I am being shown in the spirit. But, like Peter, my heart is in the right place. I know that Jesus is the Christ, the Son of the Living God. When Jesus asked for my decision, before we crossed over the bridge to that magnificent place on the mountainside, in my vision, I said to Him, "Lord, I want to be with you."

When we put our faith in the Living Christ, Jesus will walk with us and will teach us all we need to know about God and the Kingdom of Heaven, so that we may live a more productive and meaningful life here on earth.

Life is indeed difficult, and the path to inner contentment is not an easy one. In every situation there are decisions to be made and problems to overcome, as we continue our journey through life. But to get to the top of God's holy mountain, we must be willing to go where Jesus is leading us. At times the road is narrow, the climb is steep, and we go through some dark tunnels as we are traveling on the path with Jesus. But, as we learn to trust in Him, we will be comforted and will feel the presence of God's Holy Spirit in every situation in life.

9

CHALLENGES IN MARRIAGE

Therefore I prayed,
And prudence was given me;
I pleaded, and the Spirit of Wisdom came to me.

—*Wisdom 7:7*

After my recovery from foot surgery, Art and I decided I would not go back to work. Art's business was up again, and I was busy putting this book together. Hence, I took time off from my job outside the home to help Art with his construction business. At that time we were all involved in a new family project, which we thought might turn into a good money maker, so that we could all earn a living working together. Eight months after quitting my job, the economy slowed down again, Art's construction business was barely keeping the bills paid, and the family project had failed to produce as we had hoped.

Art was worried about his business and the economy. Because he was unhappy about that situation, he turned his frustrations on me. He thought I was spending too much time at my typewriter. When I first started to put this book together, Art was thrilled about the idea. He did not realize how slow a project it would be.

Art and I were like night and day in our thinking. We were divided about spiritual things. Art believed in God and in Jesus, but, in spite of his faith in God, he was not interested in reading the Bible. Art believed that if we went to church on Sunday mornings and listened attentively to what the priest was saying, then that would be enough time for God. The rest of the week we should be free to do whatever we chose. Spending time with God on a daily basis was then, as it is now, very important to me. The first hour after awakening each day is my time with God. Having quiet time to myself with God, in prayer and mediation, helps me to go through the day better equipped to face new challenges.

I don't want to give the impression that all one needs to do in life is to go to church, read the Bible, listen to sermons, and talk about God. That would be self-limiting. In my experience, however, communicating with God gives more meaning to life. Since my born-again awakening, He has given me a new lease on life. Everything I do now is done with more zest. I enjoy people, good conversation, walking, gardening, reading, taking trips, seeing the world—and I loved dancing and being with Art.

Art and I were totally different. He was more physical. He enjoyed sports. Most of what he watched on TV was boring to me. TV for Art was his way of relaxing. He was not a reader. Reading would put him to sleep. Understanding that we were different helped me learn to accept our differences. Art thought that I overdid everything. He just could not understand my way of thinking or the inner drive that compelled me to strive for more wisdom about God, myself, and others.

During the early days of my gradual unfolding, our marriage became a little bumpy. Art was having a hard time adjusting to the new woman who was so vigorously emerging. He felt that he was losing control of me—and he was! I wanted to be free to develop my own personality. At that time, he did not understand the change that was taking place in me. There were so many new, interesting things for me to do and learn in life. Yet, the more involved I became in the learning process, the farther apart we drifted. My own understanding of what was happening in our relationship helped me with that situation. Art, though, thought I did not love him anymore. His thinking that I did not love him disturbed me. I wanted to express my love for him in a special way, to draw him into the depth of my soul, to share my heart with him, so that he would readily understand my commitment and my unfailing love for him. On our seventeenth wedding anniversary, I wrote the following poem for Art:

I Love You Because You're You

I love your smile, your face and warm embrace
And all the sweet and wonderful things you do.
But, most of all I love you because you're you.
You're thoughtful, generous, and kind
And very dependable, too!
But I love you because you're you.
Yes! We are different as can be.
That anyone can plainly see;

Nevertheless, you are very important to me.
For, as the river differs from the rain
But when they have merged they become the same.
So, too, my darling, are we.
You're like the river; I'm like the sea
Your love replenishes me.
I am yours for all eternity,
For I have merged with thee.
But do not try to change me
For what I am I must be.
The river cannot change the sea;
Just love me because I'm me.
As I love you because you're you.

After Art read the poem, he looked at me and said, "These are just words. Show me how much you love me—don't just write about it."

What Art said broke my heart! I had spent weeks searching my soul for just the right words that would help him to understand how much I really loved him. I had tried to find words that would not only express my love for him but would also help him to understand that the change that was taking place in me was for my own self-improvement and had nothing to do with lack of love for him. Art just could not grasp my new way of thinking. He was baffled and could not quite comprehend the person that was unfolding.

After I quit my job, my heart was filled with joy again. Not working allowed me the time to do all the things in life that were interesting to me, and it allowed me the time to finish putting this book together. As before, however, Art felt left out of my life. I never intended to exclude Art from any part of my life, but he was just not interested in the things in which I was involved. So I left him alone to develop his own interests. To Art's way of thinking then, a wife should have been at her husband's side to comfort him and should like all the things he liked, even if it meant just sitting with him and watching TV.

One day, after Art had been in one of his bleak moods for over a week, I decided to try to help him overcome the darkness that was surrounding him. When Art was in a self-pitying mood, I would leave him alone until he decided to come out of it. I had learned how to cope with his moods from a friend who was a counselor. This friend, George Barrett, has since died, but at that time he was trying to help us understand our differences so that we could learn to live with them and continue our marriage. We had come to a point in our relationship where I knew that something had to change, I felt that I could no longer continue to live with someone, who was so completely opposed to the person I had become.

George helped me to understand that Art was using his moods to control me. Whenever Art was down, I would not do the things my spirit enjoyed doing; instead, I would try my best to talk him out of his depression. George helped me to understand that Art would never change his negative ways as long as I continued to give in to him. Art's mood was saying to me: "I want you here with me, and if you leave me like this, you really don't love me." I didn't ever want to give Art the impression that I did not care what he was feeling or thinking. But we did come to a point in our relationship where it felt like we were on a merry-go-round. We would go around and around in circles with every disagreement and never solve anything. We were getting nowhere. I was sick to death of our merry-go-round and wanted to get off. That's when I asked George if he would help us.

For years I had been trying to get Art into counseling, and he flatly refused, saying, "No one could help us. If you would change and become the kind of wife that you should be, I would be happy!" And so it went for twenty-five years of our marriage, until I felt that I just could not take any more of Art's verbal abuse. We were going through a very long, dark tunnel in our relationship when George came on the scene. Because George was a good friend to us, Art agreed to talk to George. At the beginning of our counseling, each of us saw George separately and then together.

My first counseling session with George was very interesting. I saw him a week after he had seen Art. While I was talking to George about my issues with Art, our relationship, and our marriage, George stopped me with this question: "Why do you want to continue in this marriage, Madelene? Don't you know that you could make it on your own?"

I thought about his question for a while and then answered, "Yes, George, that's true. I could make it on my own without Art. But I don't want to!"

George answered with another question: "Madelene, why do you want to continue to live with someone who is so different from you?"

I answered, with tears in my eyes, "Because I love him, George."

"You have an impossible situation on your hands, Madelene. Art will never change. He is too old to change. He does not understand who you are, and he may never learn to relate to you. How could you continue to live with someone like that?"

I looked at George, puzzled by his questions. I answered, "Impossible? George, that word is not in my vocabulary."

He burst out laughing, and then he said, "You are so right, Madelene, in your evaluation of the situation. However, change for Art at this time in his life is highly improbable."

We continued to see George for counseling for a few weeks and then stopped. Our relationship had improved, to some degree, and Art did not feel it was necessary to continue. During the time we were counseling with George, he called one evening and invited us to join him and some other good friends (the Philpotts and the Marsons) for dinner at one of George's favorite restaurants. Art really did not want to go. The Marsons, who were our houseguests at the time, were visiting from Trinidad. They helped me talk Art into joining George and our other friends for dinner. These friends, Gladys and Frank Philpott, and Beverly, George's special friend, were all waiting for us at the restaurant.

When we got to the restaurant, the Philpotts, George, and Beverly were sitting at a window table that looked out over the San Fernando Valley. The view was magnificent. We all commented on the beauty of the sparkling lights that we could see from where we were seated. We were all having a good time, except Art. We had talked him into joining us for dinner, but that's all he was going to do. Art ate, but he said very little throughout the meal. When we were through with dinner, the Philpotts, who were very dear friends of ours, invited us to their home to continue the evening. Everyone was in agreement, but Art flatly refused. He said "I'm going home to bed."

I was really having such a good time with all our friends. I hated to go home with Art, because he was again in one of his mournful states. I kissed everyone good-bye in front of the restaurant. Art said his good-byes and walked toward our car, leaving me behind.

As I was saying good-bye to George, he said to me, "Aren't you going to join us at the Philpotts', Madelene?"

"No, George, I'd better not. Art is in one of his moods again. If I go, Art will be upset with me."

George said, "Leave him alone with his mood and come with us, if that is what you really want to do."

I went over to Art, who was sitting in our car waiting for me. On the left side of the car, I spoke to him through the window. "Darling, won't you please change your mind about going over to the Philpotts' with the others? It's too early; I really don't want to end the evening yet."

Art said, "Get in the car. I am going home to bed."

I replied, "Well, I'll see you later. I'm going with the others to the Philpotts'."

Art said, "Suit yourself"

I rode with George and Beverly to the Philpotts' home. The Philpotts, the Marsons, and I enjoyed being with George, picking his brain whenever we had the opportunity to do so. We would talk about different things, but mostly the subject would be philosophical whenever I was around. I enjoyed questioning George about life in general, asking his opinion about people's behavior and trying to gain knowledge from him because of his experiences with people he had counseled. While riding with George to the Philpotts' home, I felt concerned about going without Art and explained my feelings to George. He counseled me on the necessary steps that had to be taken if I was going to break the pattern of control that Art's moods had over me.

George said, "Madelene, if you really want to help Art to grow out of his moods, you must stop giving in to him whenever he is in despair."

I asked, "How will I accomplish that, George?"

"You have taken the first step in that direction by coming with us this evening, instead of going home with Art just because he is in a bad mood. If there is something you want to do, invite Art to join you. If he refuses, go ahead and do what you have to do to develop your own personality, and enjoy life while you can. Relax, Madelene. Art will be okay, and he will learn from this experience."

Years passed, as we continued in our marriage, and Art did learn that when he was gloomy he would be left alone until he decided to come out of his mood. Until George pointed out Art's pattern of behavior, I had tried to talk Art into feeling better, trying to cheer him up and to help him see things from a different point of view. But my efforts would end in frustration.

After we stopped seeing George for counseling, things got better for a while, at least for me, because I understood what had to be done to help Art grow in understanding of his own behavior. I continued to speak to George privately on the telephone whenever I needed his advice on any particular problem in our marriage.

While I was still working at Robinsons, Art and I had had one of the biggest explosions we have ever had in our marriage. It came at a time, naturally, when Art was again in a dark place.

It was a month before Christmas, and Robinsons was having a Christmas party for all their employees. I had invited Art to the party, but he flatly refused. The party was on a Saturday evening, and that was my special weekend off. When you work in retail, there are few weekends off. Consequently, I decided again to try to talk Art out of his mood so that he would change his mind and go with me to the party.

It was early in the morning. Art was in his office working at his desk. I was reading an article in a magazine about what causes unhappiness in people. I went into the office to share the article with Art, hoping he would respond to it in a positive way. But instead, I just made things worse. We got into a big argument and said nasty things to each other.

Art looked at me, with anger on his face and resentment in his voice, as he said, "I don't know who the hell you are. You are not the girl I married."

"Take a good look. I am the same person. But the girl you married grew up, and I wish that you would also grow into a man and stop being such a baby!"

At that, Art exploded. He threw everything that was on his desk at me, and he told me to get out of his life and out of his house. I left the office in tears. In our twenty-five years of marriage, Art had never before told me to get out of his life. In the past, whenever we had an argument, he would inform me that he was going to pack his bags and leave, because no one appreciated him. When the children were little, it would scare me to think that Art might leave me. So, for years, I would try not to say anything to Art that would upset him to that point. But, after my born-again experience, I realized that I could not continue to live under those conditions. It was at that point that I began to tell Art exactly what I thought, and often it was not what he wanted to hear.

This time, it was different. Art told me that he could not stand the sight of me, and he wanted me out of his life and out of his house. I was crushed. I called George to tell him I was leaving Art. George told me to meet him at the Philpotts'. He wanted to talk to me before I decided to do anything. I agreed to meet with George. It took me half an hour to get to the Philpotts'. When I got there, George was waiting for me. The Philpotts, as always, were very gracious and accommodating. They went shopping and left me alone to speak with George. George spent three hours listening to me—I sobbed the whole time while talking to him.

I said, "George, you were so right. It's impossible. I cannot take it any more! I am leaving Art! Art gave me permission to leave him." I cried and continued to sob, as George just listened and handed me Kleenex after Kleenex until I could cry no more.

George said, "Madelene, if you leave Art, no one would blame you, and you would probably have an easier life without him. There is no doubt in my mind that you can make it on your own. But what would become of Art if you left him? What would he do without you? You are his whole life. You are everything to him."

I interrupted, "I don't want to be his everything! I can't be his everything! I'm sick to death of being Art's everything! I just want to be who I am, and I want him to know me as I am and to love me just as I am."

George agreed, "You're so right. You should not be Art's everything—but you are. And if you leave him, he would be devastated. Would you be able to live with yourself if anything should happen to Art?"

"I don't know, George," I replied. "I just don't know."

10

A VISION OF HOPE

Therefore I tell you, all that you ask for in prayer
Believe that you received it
And it shall be yours.

—*Mark 11:24*

"I want you to give this a lot of thought before you move out," George continued. "Don't just leave without thinking about all the consequences of your leaving."

"But, George, I can't go back to that house now. Art will think that everything is all right again, and that he can do or say anything to me, and I will always be there to take his garbage. I won't take any more of that from him!"

"Madelene put Art in his place! Let him know that you will not speak to him when he maltreats you. He will then learn that if he wants your attention he will have to be respectful in his behavior toward you."

"How can I go back home now and keep my dignity? Art told me in very firm language to get out of his house and out of his life. What would I say to him if I go back?"

"Madelene, the house and everything in it are half yours! You tell Art that you have given a lot of thought to leaving him. But you decided that nobody is going to throw you out of your own home. If he is unhappy, then he should leave. You know that Art would never leave you. You are the leveling force in Art's life. And you must continue to help him if you really love him."

With tears in my eyes, I said, "I want to be free, to be who I am, and to become all that I was meant to be. I have a mountain to climb, and I must continue my journey. Art just won't come with me. He is in a miserable state, feeling sorry for himself. He won't join me on my beautiful mountain, where the sun is warm and bright and everything is peaceful."

George was listening attentively, and I continued. "I have been sitting on my special mountain for years now, waiting for Art and hoping that he would look up at me and see the sun shining all around me. And, because he does love me, I thought that he would want to join me here in the sunshine, a place of warmth and beauty."

"Madelene, Art is *unable* to join you. He has been in the same position for so long that he is physically unable to move. You must come down from your mountain to help him."

"No! George, I am not moving from this place of beauty! It took me a very long time to get this far, and I'm never going back to that dreary place where Art is. I will wait for him here, where I am, but I will not go back down into his darkness."

"Madelene, you do not have to be afraid of the darkness anymore. It cannot overcome you. You have been sitting in the light on your mountain for such a long time that you have absorbed the light, and you are now a part of that light. Wherever you go now, the light will go with you, because the light is in you. You must help Art, by being the light in his life, so that he may see his way out of his own darkness. You may have to slow down your pace. He will not be able to travel as fast as you. But if you decide to go back to where Art is, he will know that you really love him, and he will want to continue the journey with you. The decision is yours, Madelene. Think about all that I have said to you."

The Philpotts came home. Gladys offered us something cold to drink and told me that I could spend the weekend with them if I wished. I thanked Gladys for being such a loving friend but said no. I had a party to go to that evening at Robinsons. I thanked George, kissed him and the Philpotts good-bye, and left for home.

As soon as I got into my car and drove out of their driveway, I began to cry again. My tears continued to flow while I drove home, praying the whole time, asking God to help me make the right decision—not only for myself, but for Art, too. I wanted to help Art. I did not want to go back to the same position we had been in before: knowing that neither Art nor I could continue to live as we had lived for all those years and not knowing what direction our marriage would take. I knew a change was necessary if we were going to continue to live together in the same house.

When I arrived at our home, my tears were still flowing. So I drove past the house and continued to drive until I reached Saint Bernardine's Church, a mile and a half away. I went inside. It was about two o'clock in the afternoon, and there was no one else in the church at that time. I entered the church by a side door and got into the first pew. I knelt down in front of the Tabernacle for a few minutes and prayed:

"Heavenly Father, please listen to my plea. Speak to me, Father. Tell me what to do. I want to do what is right, but I just don't know what is right anymore. Do you want me to leave Art? You know, Father, that I will do anything you tell me to do. Please speak to me, Father. Let me hear your voice. You know how much I love you and want to do your will."

I cried as I prayed. After a few minutes, I sat down in the pew and continued to speak to God, with sorrow in my heart. After sitting in silence for a few more minutes, I drifted off into a blissful state. I saw myself on a mountaintop, as if I were waiting for someone. I was all alone on that mountain, just sitting there. I watched myself get up from where I was seated, looking at the higher mountain ahead of me for a few minutes, and then turning around to start walking back down a path leading off the mountain. When I had moved a little way back from where I had been seated, I noticed a narrow, rough, rocky path on a steep slope of the mountainside. It led to the valley between two mountains. I started down the path, climbing backward, reaching first with one foot and then the other, and hanging on to the rocks on the path for support so that I would not lose my footing.

The rocks were cut out of the mountainside and were like very narrow steps, as I moved backward, stepping one foot after the other. I came to an open area between the two mountains. On arriving at the bottom of the mountain, I turned around and saw Art sitting there. His knees were pulled up to his chest, his arms were around his knees, and his head was bent down resting on his knees. I stood there just looking at Art and observing the spot where he was sitting. It was cold and dreary. The high mountains overshadowed where he sat so that the sun never seemed to shine there. There was nothing but rocks and dirt in that place. I just stood there for a while, looking at Art. Then I touched him on his right shoulder. He lifted his eyes to look at me but stayed in the same position. I prompted him to get up, inviting him to come with me to the top of the mountain where the sun was shining. I pointed to the rocky path on the side of the mountain and told him it was a shortcut back up to the top where I had been waiting for him to join me.

The look of surprise on his face told me he had not expected to see me there. He dropped his arms to the ground, as he pushed, trying to get on his feet. He was unable to move. I took hold of his hands and pulled on him, trying to help him get on his feet. He was unable to stand and fell back in the same position as before. The expression on his face showed his frustration. He was really trying to stand up but could not seem to get his body to move.

I became concerned and thought, *"Lord, now what? I came back to help Art, but he is unable to stand by himself, and he is too heavy for me to carry."*

While I was speaking to the Lord in prayer and looking up at the mountain that I had just descended, two angels appeared. They were flying down toward us. They landed in front of me, one on each side of Art. One angel grabbed Art under his left shoulder, while the other took his right shoulder. Together they lifted him out of his seated position. The angels flew back up to the mountains over the rocky path, carrying Art by the shoulders, and I followed them, walking on my own up the path. When we got back to the path on the mountain where I had been seated at the start of the vision, the angels put Art down and said to me, "He's all yours now. Good luck." When I looked back, they had disappeared!

Art was very wobbly; it looked as if he could not stand on his own, so I grabbed hold of him, putting his right arm around my shoulder, holding his right arm with my right hand, and putting my left arm around his waist. As I did that, I looked down at the place where Art had been seated and saw what seemed to be an empty shell. Then I understood that the angels had pulled Art out of the shell, which had been a shelter to him for many years. I also realized that Art would need my help and support until he was able to stand on his own. The vision ended. I came out of prayer and sat in the pew for a few more minutes. People were filtering in and out of the church for confession. I looked at my watch and realized an hour and fifteen minutes had elapsed since my entrance into the church.

I said in prayer, *"Okay, Lord. I know now what you want me to do. Please help me to say and do only what is right. Speak your words through me, and stay with me. Be my strength, so that I may help Art find his way back to you."*

On my arrival home, it was about four o'clock in the afternoon. Art was sitting in his office looking at television. Noelle and Dennis were with him. I walked past his office, not saying anything to anyone. By the time I got into my bedroom,

This painting represents the beautiful place that I would go to in my imagination during my quiet time in meditation. It's where I saw myself sitting in the vision I had in church, before I returned home to Art to continue our marriage.

Dennis was there with me. He came up behind me, embraced me, and said, "Mom, I'm so happy you came back. Dad thought you had left for good. He thought he really blew it this time."

I did not answer Dennis but started to cry again. Dennis continued, "Mom, are you all right? I'm sorry, Mom, and Dad is sorry, too. You know how Dad is. He did not mean anything he said to you."

I was holding Dennis with both my arms around his shoulders, as he hugged me tight, with his arms around my waist. Dennis has always been there for me. Whenever I was unhappy, even when he was a very young child, he was the one who would always come to me whenever he saw me cry. After a while, Dennis left me alone in my room. I had decided while driving home from church to go to the Christmas party at Robinsons without Art. While I was trying to find something to wear to the party, Noelle came into the bedroom.

"Mom I'm going out to get something for dinner, and Dad wanted me to ask you what you would like to eat. Would you like me to get some fried chicken, or would you prefer something else?"

I looked at Noelle and said, "Get whatever Dad wants. I'm going out for dinner."

Noelle asked, "Where are you going?"

"Out I have a date!"

Noelle came over and hugged me, saying, "Dad is really sorry for all the bad things he said to you today. You know how much he really loves you. He has been crying since you left this morning. That's why Dennis and I have been talking to him and staying with him. He is hurting too, Mom. When we were little, and Dad would say things to us that he did not mean, you would tell us how much he really loved us, and would try to explain that Dad could not help himself whenever he got upset. So you know that's true, Mom. Dad needs your help. You must help him; you can't leave him. He would not want to live without you."

I looked at Noelle, pulled away from her, started to cry again, and said, "Why must it always be me? I can't help him. He must help himself. I'm sick and tired of always trying to help him. He must stand on his own feet. I cannot carry him anymore, and I'm not going to!"

Noelle put her arms around my shoulders and said, "Mom, don't say that. You know that you must help him."

I pushed Noelle's arms away from my shoulders and said, "Why? Why must I? What about your father? Why don't you talk to him about helping me? I need help, too!"

"I know you do, Mom, but you know Dad won't listen to anyone. But, he will listen to you, now, if you will talk to him, because he really doesn't want you to leave. Life would be over for Dad if you left. You can't leave!"

"Why can't I leave? I'm free to do whatever is in my heart. Your father told me to get the hell out of his house and his life!"

Noelle answered, "Yes, we know, Mom. Dennis and I know all that Dad said to you, and he *is* sorry. He told us so!"

"So! Dad is sorry! What's new? He is always sorry after he hurts me! But why should I keep taking it from him? It's time for him to get some of his own medicine."

"Don't talk that way, Mom!"

"Why shouldn't I? Why must it always be me to give in?"

"Because you know better," Noelle said. "You understand things in a way that Dad can't understand. And if you don't help him, no one will!" With that, Noelle left the room.

I continued to cry, thinking that Noelle was on Art's side. At the same time, I asked myself why it was always like that. Our children, Michael, Dennis, and Noelle, would always say to me whenever I was upset with Art, "Mom, you know how Dad is. He didn't mean what he said! But you should know better!"

Why should I always be the one to know better? I continued to cry, feeling sorry for myself. Why isn't anyone on my side? Even George is on Art's side. What do I have to do to let people know that I have feelings too, that I'm just a human being with flesh and blood like anyone else?

After an hour of sobbing and self-pity, I took a shower, got dressed, and left the room. Art, Dennis, and Noelle were sitting at the kitchen table, eating, talking, and laughing, as if everything was all right again. I thought to myself, *"Look at them! Life for me is falling apart, and they don't even seem to care!"* As I walked past the kitchen, Noelle and Dennis looked at me. Art did not.

Noelle said "You look nice, Mom. Have a good time! Say hello to everyone for me."

I realized then that they all knew my destination; Art obviously had told them. I did not answer Noelle and walked out the front door without saying a word to anyone. I hoped in my heart that they would get the message; I wanted everyone to know that I was upset! In the past, if I'd been angry with Art, I would still have spoken to our children. But this time I was too upset to talk to anyone. I wanted them to know that I had feelings, too.

While I drove to the Robinsons party, my thoughts were reflecting back on the events of the day. I remembered all George had said to me and the vision at church. I could see Art in my mind's eye, trying to get up but falling back into the same seated position, the angels picking him up and placing him on the mountaintop. With that, I started praying again, just speaking to God, and asking Him to help me— and Art, too.

"I know that Art is hurting, Lord," I said. "He is like a little boy, always wanting his way, thinking that if I would do everything just the way he thinks it should be done, he would be happy. You know, Lord, how hard it is to be a good wife to Art. I can never seem to satisfy him. As soon as I start being myself with him, he gets upset with me."

My praying stopped when I began to analyze Art's behavior. I realized that there was something missing in Art's life, something that was causing him so much unhappiness. Art expected me to satisfy his every need. Yet, I could not be everything to Art. As much as I loved him, he was not everything to me. There was so much in life that I enjoyed doing by myself or with others. Art just could not understand how I could enjoy doing anything without him. As I was praying and pleading for help, better understanding came to me. I realized then that I could not help Art. Someone who was a lot wiser than both of us would have to help us.

11

RECALLING OUR BEGINNING

Charm is deceptive. And beauty is fleeting
(But) a woman who fears the Lord is to be praised!

—*Proverbs 31:30*

When I arrived at Robinsons, the party was in full swing. I joined Minica Bond and some of our other friends at their table for dinner. There was music playing, and people were dancing and having a wonderful time. I thought to myself, "What a shame Art isn't here." We both love to dance, and that's the one thing we do have in common.

My mind then flashed back to our very first meeting, which had been in a ballroom. While I was dancing with someone else, Art had cut in on us. It was a cheat dance, an opportunity for everyone in the ballroom to cheat on whomever they wanted to dance with; otherwise, some people would have just sat there on the side, maybe not getting even one dance all evening. Shortly after Art cut in on the young man with whom I was dancing, the music stopped. I was relieved! Cheat dances were not my favorite. I liked having the option of saying no. But if you were dancing and someone cut in on your partner during a cheat dance, you would be stuck with him until the music ended. After the music stopped, I excused myself and walked off the dance floor. As I was walking away, Art said, "Where are you going? We did not get to dance much."

"Sorry, but I have to go to the ladies' room!" I stayed in the ladies' room for half an hour, until I thought the cheat dance had ended. As I came down the steps from the ladies' room, Art was standing at the foot of the stairway. He said, "Shall we finish that dance now?"

I stopped for a minute, as I listened to the music that was being played, and I said to him, "That's a rumba. Do you know how to rumba?"

He answered, "I can try!"

By this time, he had taken hold of my left hand and was walking ahead of me toward the dance floor. I followed him, but I was thinking, "*If he can't do a rumba, I will walk off the dance floor!*"

As we started to dance, I was pleasantly surprised! He was actually doing the rumba! I could hardly believe that I had met an American who could do the rumba. I had been in Los Angeles for three years and had gone to many dances, but that was the first time I had met anyone who knew the difference between a foxtrot and a rumba!

I asked Art, "Where did you learn to dance like this?"

"I am a dancer and dance instructor," he answered.

I was so excited that I had finally met someone who could dance the way I like to dance. I immediately took Art over to meet my mother, Rosa, and my girlfriend, Vivian. They were delighted. For the rest of the evening, Art danced exclusively with the three of us. At the end of the evening we said good-bye and thanked him for dancing with us. We told him we would be back again next Saturday night.

He asked, "Do you always come to this ballroom?

"No, but we had such a good time dancing with you; we will be back again next week for more good dancing!"

He responded, "Well, I guess I'll see you then."

The following Saturday evening, Art was waiting for us when we arrived. He came up to us and said, "You're late! I thought maybe you had changed your mind about coming."

We said, "Well, we're here now, so let's dance!"

Art danced with me first. He danced next with my mother and then with Vivian. At the end of the evening, he offered to take us home. We agreed, because it was raining. Art stopped at a drive-in restaurant on the way home and got us all hot chocolate. When we arrived at my mother's home, I was the last one out of the car. As I was getting out, Art said, "I don't have your phone number."

I looked at him and replied, "It's in the phone book."

Mother answered, "No, it isn't!" And she gave him our phone number.

When we got into the house, I asked Mother, "Why did you give him our unlisted telephone number? We don't even know him."

"I know, but he's nice. I like him."

The next Saturday, Art called while I was at a Christmas party. He spoke to Mother, but was disappointed that I was not at home; she invited him to come to the house the next day for dinner. That's the way it began. We met on the third Saturday of November 1954 and were married a year later in November 1955.

While I was sitting at the dinner table at Robinsons, deep in thought, Minica interrupted me by asking, "Madelene, are you all right?"

"No, I'm not. Can we go somewhere quiet after the party for coffee? I need to talk with you." At the end of the party, Minica and I said good-bye to our friends and left the building together. Minica offered to drive and asked where I'd like to go. I suggested a coffee shop a few blocks from Robinsons. When we got to the restaurant, we both ordered coffee and pie. I related to Minica all that had transpired that day and what Art had said to me that morning. I told her about my meeting with George, the vision I had had in church, and what had happened when I returned home from church. I shared with Minica all that was on my mind and explained the feelings that were in my heart.

Minica asked, "What do you think that vision is trying to convey to you, Madelene?"

"I believe that God is telling me through that vision that I must help Art to stand on his own." Then I said, "But if we are going to continue to live together, there must be a change. We cannot live under these conditions any longer. I'm sick to death of Art's moods."

Minica asked, "How are you going to implement a change in Art's attitude, Madelene?"

"I really don't know. But God knows, and He will guide me."

I related to Minica what Art had told me the first time we were alone, without my mother and Vivian. For the first few weeks after Art came to our home for dinner, whenever we went dancing, he would include Mother and Vivian. On New Year's Eve, six weeks after we met, Art proposed to me.

I laughed and said, "You have got to be kidding! You don't even know me!" Up to that point in our relationship, we had never been alone on a date. It was 2:00 am, New Year's Day, 1955, and we were alone for the first time in my mother's living room. The four of us had just gotten back from a dance. Mother and Vivian had said good night to us and gone to bed.

Vivian lived alone. She and I worked together at a cafeteria in downtown Los Angeles, so whenever we were out together late, she would always sleep over at my house and go to her own apartment the next day. My mother was still married to her second husband, Bill Hinkle. Bill didn't like to dance, and Mother did, so Vivian and I would invite her to go with us whenever we went dancing.

Now, for the first time since we'd met, Art and I were finally alone—and he proposed to me. I could not believe that he was serious, and I told him so. As far as I was concerned, he was fun to be with, but he was just a friend to all three of us. He had kissed me for the first time that evening because it was New Year's Eve! Everyone in the night club was kissing and hugging! He kissed my mother and Vivian, too, at the club. But now in the living room, we kissed again, as we said good night.

After he proposed to me, he told me that from the very moment when he first saw me in the ballroom, he knew he was going to marry me.

I laughed loudly and said, "Surely you must be joking!"

He answered, "No, I'm not".

"But how could you think you were going to marry me, when you had not even met me?"

"That was the closest thing I've ever had to a religious experience!"

I asked him what he meant by that. Art explained it this way: "For three weeks before you came into that ballroom, I would go there every Saturday night, looking for someone to train as a dance partner, but I never saw anyone who interested me. So, I just sat there each week and watched everyone dance however, when *you* entered the ballroom that evening, I heard a voice in my head that said, *"That's her! She's the one! Don't let her get away from you!"* Art continued, "From that moment on, I have never been able to get you out of my mind. As a matter of fact, I forgot my reason for going to the ballroom in the first place! I went there looking for someone to train as a dance partner, but, instead, I found you—the girl I'm going to marry; the girl I have been waiting for all my life!"

He continued, "It is really funny now, as I think about that experience, and even talking about it gives me goose bumps all over. I don't really understand it myself. All I know is," he said again, "You are the girl I have been waiting for all my life."

I knew that Art was telling me the truth, as he was speaking from his heart. There were tears in his eyes as he related that experience to me. He continued to speak, and I just listened, fascinated by what he was saying. He continued, "The strange thing is, I could not see your face as you came into the ballroom, but when I saw you up close, you had the face that I had seen many times in my mind—the face of the girl that I would marry!"

I asked Art to tell me something about himself. He shared his life story with me. He was the eleventh of twelve children. His mother had died when he was just eight years old. His father left the family without any means of support. Art's oldest brother, Michael, and his next-oldest sister, Elizabeth, quit school as teenagers, got jobs, and kept the family together, with the help of the state.

Art's parents had been emigrants from Hungary. Before Art started school, he had spoken and understood only Hungarian. As I listened to Art's life story, my heart went out to him. Speaking about his past life made Art seem like such a little boy to me. I realized then that Art really needed someone to love him, and he had selected me for the job.

Art continued with his story. He told me that his brother, Michael, and sister, Elizabeth, were like father and mother to him. When his father deserted the family, the state had wanted to put the young children into an orphanage. But Michael and Elizabeth both agreed to help by going to work, if the state would let the family stay together. That was during the Depression, in the state of Ohio, where Art was born and lived until he entered the service at the age of twenty.

Art then stopped talking about himself and said, "Well! Now that you know my life story, will you marry me?"

I laughed and said, "Ask me again in six months, and I will give you my answer then!"

Art said, "Okay, I will!" By this time it was four o'clock in the morning. We had been sitting on my mother's sofa in the living room, telling each other our life stories. Realizing how late is was, I said, "Look what time it is—I have to get to bed!" He apologized to me for keeping me up so late, and left for home.

"That's our story, Minica."

"That's a very interesting story, Madelene. You are probably the one that God sent into Art's life as a light that will lead him and help him to find his own path to God."

"But, Minica, Art thinks *I'm* his god. He expects me to be his everything. You know that only God can satisfy the hunger that's in our hearts, the need to feel loved. No one but God can do that. If Art would only surrender his needs to God, God would fill him with His love. Then Art would feel better about himself and life in general. He would also understand that I *do* love him."

"Minica, I just can't seem to love Art in the way he expects me to love him. It is so frustrating always having to prove myself with him. Every time I do anything that helps me to understand more about the person that I am, Art takes that separation from him as a sign that I don't love him.

"Art has never separated himself from me to see himself as his own person. He thinks that if I stop breathing, life would end for him, too. I can't seem to help him to see things as they really are and not as he perceives them to be."

"You must continue to be the light in Art's life, Madelene. You know, Jesus told us that we must be the light of the world. When we act and think like Jesus, the world will see His light in us. You must be Jesus to Art, and then he will follow you into God's Kingdom. I will be praying for you. But let's pray together now."

Minica prayed with me for a few minutes, asking God to be with me as I went back home to be with Art. She asked God's Holy Spirit to work through me to help Art and our marriage. I thanked Minica for taking the time to care and for being there for me in my time of need. Minica drove me back to where we had left my car in the Robinsons parking lot. We said good-bye, and I left for home.

As I drove home, my mind was racing back and forth, remembering all the happy times in our lives together, and recalling the unhappy events of that day. I also thought about what I had said to George when he told me to go back home and to tell Art that the house was mine, too, and that no one was going to throw me out of my own home! I had answered George, "Well, if I do go back to the house, I'm going to sleep on the couch until Art apologizes to me."

George said, "That's nonsense, Madelene. Why should you be uncomfortable sleeping on a couch while Art is comfortably sleeping in his bed? Half the bed belongs to you, so sleep on your side of the bed!"

"George, you really don't know Art. He is going to think that all is well again. He will expect me to be receptive to him and will want to make love to me. That's just the way Art is."

George replied, "You don't always have to do what Art expects you to do to be a good wife to him. Don't let him intimidate you by his words and actions. If you don't want him to touch you until he apologizes, then tell him so. Communicate your feelings to him. You can't just assume that Art knows what you are thinking. Don't let your feelings control you. Let go of the anger that you feel toward Art, and help him to get in touch with his feelings. Teach Art through your actions and behavior."

George continued, "Think of all we have discussed today. Give it some time to soak in. If, after giving it a lot of thought, you decide that the challenge is greater than you can handle, I will understand, and I will help you to live with your decision."

When I arrived home from Robinsons, everyone was in bed. It was 1:00 am. I went into our bathroom to get ready for bed. I could hear Art moving and knew that he was still awake. When I was through getting ready for bed, I went into our bedroom and got into my side of the bed.

We had a king-size bed, so I laid on the very edge of my side, as far away from Art as possible. But, as always, Art touched me with his foot. Whenever we had a disagreement and Art was sorry for his behavior toward me, his routine was to touch me with his foot when we were in bed. That was his way of saying that he was sorry and telling me by his actions that he wanted me near him, so that he could make love to me.

In the past, I had usually given in to his advances, so that he would start the next day in a better mood. Thus, for the first few years of our marriage, I had said nothing, keeping my feelings to myself and resenting Art for his behavior toward me. Life had become a hell for me. I had been sick all the time. I had suffered from headaches, lived on aspirins, and developed ulcers. Life had been so miserable for me that I had wanted to die. It was then, at my lowest point that Jesus had come into my life. And the person that I *was* did, indeed, die.

That person who was so afraid to live was resurrected into a new life. Jesus called me out of my own darkness into His light of love and forgiveness, which helped me to see that it was okay to be me. When I recovered from my illness, a different person emerged. That's when I began to express my feelings freely to Art, as I ascended to the top of God's holy mountain.

Climbing a mountain is not an easy task. There are many obstacles to overcome before we can reach the top. Consequently, I knew exactly what George was trying to tell me, and I accepted the challenge. The following pictures are of Art and me having fun through the years: dancing, cruising, and just enjoying our life together.

In Loving Memory of My Dear Friend Minica Bond
1933–1998

A Friend

Whatever befalls us, we can bear
If we have a friend standing there
To hold our hand and see us through
Life's difficult moments that make us blue;
You were there when I needed you
Your hand touching mine, a friend in a crisis;
You helped me through that difficult time.
Thank you, friend, for giving so much Love and support with just a simple
touch.
Whatever befalls us, we can bear
If we have a friend standing there!

—*by Gloria Jean Hill*
Palm Springs, CA

Thanks, Minica, for all your prayers and caring friendship. You were an angel to me throughout our earthly friendship. I miss you! Please continue to pray for me, until I'm with you again in our heavenly home.

12

CLIMBING A MOUNTAIN IN OUR RELATIONSHIP

Come; let us climb the Lord's mountain
To the house of the God of Jacob
That he may instruct us in his ways
And we may walk in his paths.

—Isaiah 2:3

Art gently touched my leg with his foot, in silence, saying nothing to me. I pulled my whole body closer to the edge of the bed, barely having enough room to hang on to the side. Art touched me again, rubbing my leg with his foot, still saying nothing. I kicked and pushed his foot away from me. He got the message and left me alone, and he finally fell asleep. As I lay there, with my mind racing back and forth, remembering the good and bad times in our relationship, I asked God again to help us in our journey together and to show us the way to work out our differences.

The next morning was Sunday, so, as usual; I went directly into the shower and got ready for church. As I was leaving for church, Art was sitting in his favorite chair watching TV. I stopped in the hallway in front of his office and said to him in a firm voice, "We need to talk."

Art answered with a smile in his voice, as he said, "Okay."

I continued, "Are you going to be here when I get home from church?"

He replied, "I'm not going anywhere."

His voice was sweet, and I could tell that he was out of his dark mood. When Art was not in a bad mood, he was fun to be with. Art had qualities that I really admire in a man. He was dependable, trustworthy, honest, and he had a soft and compassionate heart. He was a good father. Our children and I were Art's whole life. He wanted our children to have everything they needed, things he himself did not have as a child. Sometimes Art would go overboard, trying to make up for his lost childhood by being a child with our children. In order to provide for all that we needed as a family, Art had two jobs. He worked as a carpenter in the daytime and as a dance instructor at night.

The first few years after our children came into our lives, we could not afford to take vacations. As years passed, however, things got a little better financially. Art's construction business was providing for us. One day, he came home with a small trailer. Our children were so excited! We lived in a neighborhood where most of our neighbors went camping with their families. Our children would ask us why we didn't go camping. It would break Art's heart if the children wanted anything that he felt he could not provide for them. His concern was not only for our children, but for me, too. If I was out with Art, window shopping, and stopped to admire anything, Art would want to buy it for me. That's the kind of person Art was. He always wanted us to have whatever we wanted.

Nonetheless, when Art brought the trailer home, we got into an argument. I thought we could not afford it. It was always like that. Art would spend money, and I would get upset. To Art, buying things made him feel good and provided excitement for the moment. Then, at the end of the month when the bills would come in, Art would be depressed again, and I would have to live with his unhappiness. To me, it just wasn't worth having something if we would have to worry about paying for it later. Our children did not see it that way. They saw me as a "fun spoiler"—and that's the way it was with us, for years.

Now, in retrospect, I could see that I must have made life miserable for Art, too. He was trying so hard to be a good husband to me and the best father he could be to our children. The problem was in our differences. We were both insecure in our behavior, but we expressed our insecurities in different ways. In looking back, I can see now that getting that little trailer was really a good idea. We had some of the best times together as a family on our many camping trips taken in that trailer.

I know now that Art really loved me. But there was a time in our marriage when I did not feel loved, not from Art, nor from anyone else. My low self-esteem made me feel that I had to prove myself to everyone, because I wanted so much to be loved. The problem was my own insecurities. Now I know that "God is love" and that He dwells in my heart, and He is the master of my soul. No one can take that away from me or destroy His love, which has become a part of me. God's love is perfecting and uplifting. When we can feel the embrace of His love in our lives, the feeling of contentment fills us with joy. Then love flows from us into the lives of others.

I thought of all these things while driving to church and wondered also where I had failed Art. I decided that leaving Art alone for so long a time to discover God's love on his own had not been a good idea. I realized, at that moment, that I had to help Art find his own way to God's perfecting love. While pondering all these thoughts in my mind, I began to understand why Art felt so lost and alone, abandoned by me, the one he loved so much and wanted by his side.

I could see then why Art felt that God had taken me away from him. And because Art felt that God had taken me away from him, Art would have nothing to do with God. As I entered the church, I offered the Mass for Art, asking God to touch him with His love, so that he would understand how much he really was loved. I also asked God to work through me, so that I might express His perfect love to Art in a way that Art could understand. I asked God also to heal me of my hurts and to take away any pain that might still be there from what Art had said to me the day before. I asked Him to heal Art of all the pain that he was experiencing because of my behavior toward him.

My thoughts drifted then to wondering how I must have looked to Art from where he was sitting. He must have thought of me as someone who was looking down on him, I understood then that all I had done had not been to help Art. It had been for my own self-improvement and coming into a better understanding of who I was and what love really was. I knew that all that had happened thus far was preparing me to help Art grasp the real meaning of God's love. I knew that it was going to be a difficult job. But I accepted the challenge and asked God to help me with my commitment to love. I realized that, when we love, we must be willing to do anything for the people we love. When we really love, we should not let fear prevent our doing what is right. Sometimes, however, when we do what is right, the people whom we love may turn against us. In spite of that, it is our responsibility to always help them in whatever way we can. I prayed that God would put the right words into my mouth, so that I could help Art come into a better understanding of where we had to go in our relationship.

When I got home from church, Art was still sitting in his favorite chair, watching a football game on TV. I walked into the office and asked him if he would like to talk now or after breakfast.

Art responded with, "After breakfast."

"Would you like to go out to eat?"

He replied, "Yes, but let's wait until after halftime."

I said okay and left the room.

At halftime, Art put on his shoes, and we went to a restaurant in our neighborhood, where we would often go for breakfast after church on Sundays. During the meal we said nothing of importance to each other. We talked about the food, the football game, and church. We were pleasant to one another, as if nothing had happened that was different in our relationship.

In the past, that's the way it would have gone until the next time we got into an argument. We would both avoid discussing our hurts, because we did not want to start up again. Our feelings would be buried, and resentment would build up in us. Consequently, we just sat there eating, as if the blowup had never taken place the day before. I knew that this time we had to discuss our feelings. I had to turn Art around, so he could understand the depth of my thoughts and the sorrow in my soul because of our broken relationship.

When we arrived back at the house, I went into the bathroom, and Art went back into his office. When I was through in the bathroom, I came out to find Art sitting in front of the TV, watching the football game.

I went into the office and said to Art, "We have to talk."

Art answered, "After the game."

I said "No! We need to talk now."

Art turned off the volume on the TV. Then, with the picture still on, he said; "Okay. Go ahead. I'm listening."

I replied, "I'm not going to talk to you while you are looking at TV."

He then turned off the TV and said, "Okay, I'm all ears; talk."

I said then, "Let's go in the living room."

Art answered, "Why? I'm comfortable here in this chair. Talk. I'm listening."

I answered in a firm voice and said, "I don't want to talk to you in this room."

I did not want to talk to Art in that room, because that was the same room in which we had had the argument the day before. I felt we needed a change of scenery.

Art replied, with sarcasm in his voice, "Yes, ma'am; whatever you say!"

He answered me as if he were speaking to his drill sergeant. I ignored his tone of voice and walked out of his office, through the living room, and out onto the patio in the backyard. It was a beautiful day, and I felt that we both needed some fresh air. Our backyard was beautiful, and we had had some fun times out there, dancing with friends and enjoying our family. Art followed me and sat down on a redwood bench that he had built around our patio. That bench was not a very comfortable place to sit, but it would serve as extra seating when we would have a dance party out there.

I asked Art to sit in a more comfortable chair, but he told me, "This is where I want to sit."

I said, "Okay, if you want to be uncomfortable, it's your choice."

Art sat there, leaning forward, holding on to the bench with his hands, one on each side of him. His feet were crossed on the ground in front of him, and his head hung down, as he looked at his feet.

He seemed so sad, like a little boy who was being scolded. Standing in front of him, I began to speak. "Art, I have given a lot of thought about leaving you, but I have decided against it. It is not my desire to leave you or this house. Half of this house and everything in it belongs to me. But there must be some changes made around here. You are going to have to accept me the way I am. It is not possible for me to be someone else. I am a mature woman now, but I'm still the same person you married. I have grown in better understanding of myself and life in general. I realize now that I can't make you happy. Therefore, I'm not going to try to make you happy anymore. You must understand that only God can make us happy. Ask God to help you."

Art looked up at me and said, "God will have nothing to do with me. He has taken you away from me"

In a soft voice, I replied, "Darling, God did not take me away from you. He has sent me back to you, and He is speaking to you now, through me. He wants you to know that He loves you as much as He loves me. The only difference between us is that I know how much I'm loved, and I accept His love. I'm trying now to share His love with you. But you must accept me as I am. God is a very important part of me. You cannot have me without God. You cannot separate me from God. God is in me, and He is also in you. You need to get to know God, if you want to understand me and yourself. He is the only one that can make us happy. No one else can do that for us."

Art answered, "If you were the kind of wife that you should be, I would be happy."

I said then, "I'm sorry Art, that I am not the kind of wife that you think I should be. And I know that you are unhappy with me as a wife. But I am who I am. I'm trying to be the best person I can be in all areas of my life. And I have really tried. God knows how hard I've tried to be the kind of wife you want me to be. But it seems that, no matter how hard I try, I can never satisfy you. So I'm not going to even try anymore. I will continue to do whatever I need to do to become all that God is calling me to be. Your being upset with me is not going to stop me from reading the Bible, going to church, or doing whatever else I must do to become a better person. You are just going to have to change your way of thinking if we are going to continue our life together."

"Why do I have to change?" Art asked. "What about you? You need to change, too."

I answered, "Because it is you, Art, who is so unhappy. To become happy, all you have to do is change your thinking and stop blaming me, and everything else, for your unhappiness. We are as happy as we make up our minds to be."

Art said, "But you don't like to do any of the things I like to do. What would be so wrong with you watching the football game with me on TV?"

I said, "Nothing. But you know I don't like football or TV. "However," I continued, "if you would take me to a football game, I would be happy to go with you. Because then it would be something we would be doing together. Not just watching TV."

Art said, "But why should I fight the traffic and sit in an uncomfortable seat, when I could be more comfortable at home watching it on TV?"

I said then, "Okay. I will make a deal with you. I will watch football on TV with you, if you will go to a Bible class with me."

Art replied, "Why should I go to a Bible class? I'm not interested in the Bible."

"That's what I'm trying to get across to you, Art." I said, "We're different! So we don't enjoy everything the other is interested in. That's okay. That does not mean we don't love each other. I have never accused you of not loving me just because you do not like to do all the things I like to do. And you're not the kind of husband I expected either! But I take the good with the bad, and I am trying to make it better."

Then I began to cry again, as I walked off the patio, back into the living room, and sat down in my favorite chair. My sobbing was uncontrollable. I remembered all the things Art had promised me when he asked me to marry him. He had told me that he loved me so much that he would never do anything to hurt me. He wanted to take care of me and make things right in life for me. I believed him, and through the years, although I had been hurt many times by him, I had never accused him of not loving me. What was hurting me now was the fact that I could not seem to make him understand how much I did love him and wanted to help him.

After a few minutes, Art came in from the backyard and came over to me. He knelt down on the floor in front of me, putting his arms around me and his head on my chest under my chin.

He said, "I'm sorry, darling. Don't cry anymore. I'm such a fool. Please forgive me." As he said that, he began to cry. I stopped crying then and put my hands on his head, saying, "Don't you start now."

He said, "I never wanted to hurt you. I love you too much to ever hurt you. I don't know why I'm so bullheaded. I could kick myself for being such a fool. If you left me, my life would be over. I would not want to live without you."

I recalled then what Art had told my mother after I broke off from seeing him three months after he had proposed to me.

Before I started dating Art, I asked him one night if he had ever been married. He said no, that he had never been married.

I asked him, "How is it that you were never married? You are thirty-two years old."

He answered, "Because I have been waiting for you all my life."

I had just told Art about seeing someone who had also proposed to me. Art had asked me, "So, why didn't you marry him?"

I answered, "Because I would never marry anyone who had been married before."

That's when I asked Art if he had ever been married. Without even a hesitation, he answered, "No."

Three months after we were dating, I found out from Art's ex-dance partner that he had indeed been married before! When I found out, I was very upset and told Art I did not want to ever see him again. But Art was persistent. He would not give in to my rejection. Art would call on the telephone every night and speak to my mother. Back then, I worked as a checker in a cafeteria, on Broadway in downtown Los Angeles. My hours were from noon to nine in the evening. During the time of my refusal to speak to Art (even on the telephone), he would come down to where I worked each night and park his car in front of the cafeteria so that he could see me. I would walk right past him, as if I didn't even know him, and take the bus. After I got off the bus, I would have to walk six dark blocks to my house. Art would drive behind me until I got into the house, not saying a word to me. After I was in the house, he would call on the telephone and speak to my mother. He told her that the reason he followed me was to make sure I got home safely.

The neighborhood where we lived was not a very safe place for a young woman to be walking alone after dark. Art's routine continued for over a month. Still, I would not even look at him or speak to him. One night, on the telephone, he told my mother that if I did not speak to him soon that he would end his life! My mother tried to get me to speak to him then, but I still refused to acknowledge him. About five weeks after I broke off with Art, I came out of work one night and Art's car was not in front of the cafeteria. He was nowhere around. "

"Well," I thought, "he finally got the message."

When I got home, Art was speaking to my mother on the telephone. He was explaining to Mother why he had not been there to see me safely home. That day he had fallen off a scaffold from a two-story apartment building he was working on, and he had sprained both his ankles! I was sorry to hear what had happened to him, but I still would not speak to him on the phone.

Mother said, "Come on, Mags! Don't be that way. What harm would it do for you to speak to him on the phone?" as she was reaching out with the phone to me.

I ignored her and said, "No! Mom, I don't want to speak to him."

She then asked, in a firm voice, while still holding the phone out to me, "What kind of Christian are you?"

With that remark from Mother, I took the phone out of her hand and said "Hello".

So there we were, twenty-five years later, making up again after I had been ready to leave Art and go on with my life. When we finally stopped crying, I shared with Art the vision I had had in church the day before, and I told him that I had come back to help him climb the mountain. I also took him over to a picture I had painted of my mountain many years before. I showed him where I had been sitting on that mountain and the place between the two mountains where I had seen him sitting in my vision. That was the end of that crisis. Art started going to church with me on Sundays when we were getting along, but if he was upset with me, he would not go. He was trying a new method of control, but that didn't work for him, either.

Here we are two years later, in a new crisis. I have quit my job, with Art's approval. However, like so many of those stormy times before, Art is upset with me. He thinks I'm giving too much time to writing this book and not enough time to him. It was at this point that I saw myself with Jesus, on that special mountain where He introduced me to Saint Peter. I was confused about that vision and prayed about it night and day, asking God to help me to know what to do. I was wondering if the vision meant that I should move out of the house, so that I would be free to work on the book whenever I had the opportunity, without Art being around to get upset with me.

One day during that period of time, Art and I had another explosion in our relationship. In anger, I took the initiative and told Art that I had had enough of his bad moods and that I could not stand living with his unhappiness any longer. I told him that I had decided to move out as soon as I could go back to work. I was definitely serious about moving out, believing *that* was the meaning of my call to be with the Lord. If the Lord was calling me to be with Him, that's where I wanted to be, even if it meant ending our marriage. I moved out of our bedroom into the rumpus room and took my typewriter and pillow with me. I stayed there for two weeks. Whenever Art would come home from work he would find me at the typewriter, diligently and persistently working on this book.

My progress was slow. My heart was in the right place. My lack of literary skills and poor spelling ability got in the way. Nevertheless, I continued to work at it night and day. Because Art was upset with me anyway, I did not feel I had to stop working at the typewriter whenever he came home. I would take time out, however, to check the newspaper for work and a place to move into. I knew that I would not be able to afford my own apartment on my salary. So I was looking for a room in someone's home, maybe a widow or a divorcee, or a working woman who had to support herself and needed someone to share expenses.

I called my friend, Minica Bond, to tell her what was happening and to share my vision with her.

Minica asked me, "Would you consider going back to work at Robinsons?"

I said, "No, I would probably go back to the new store."

Minica asked, "Why, Madelene? I thought you didn't like working there."

I answered, "I hate it there!"

"Then why would you go back there, Madelene?" Minica asked.

I answered, "Because I can make the most money there. Now that I have decided to leave Art, and would have to support myself, I could learn to like working there."

Minica said, "Well, Madelene, I'll be praying for you."

"Thanks, Minica. I need all the prayers that I can get."

While driving home, I prayed, "Heavenly Father, *I'm scared to death! Help me to really know what to do. I don't really want to leave Art, but if that's what you want me to do, I will do it. Father, just give me the strength and the courage to go through with it. And, Father, I really don't want to go back to work in that stressful place. You know my feelings about going back to work there! But if that's where you want me to work, Lord, I will work there. I want to do Thy will, Father. Just help me to know what your will is for me. Lord, please speak to me, so that I may understand. Take away this confusion from my mind. Let Your will be clear to me."* My prayers continued until I arrived home.

13

A New Awakening

The people who walked in darkness
Have seen a great light;
Upon those who dwelt in the land of gloom
A light has shone.

—Isaiah 9:2

On my arrival home from my meeting with Minica, I went directly into our bedroom and sat down in my meditation chair to continue in prayer. In meditation, I was once again walking with Jesus on the mountain. On our journey together, I was learning a lot from Jesus. One day we were on a beautiful path that seemed to be leading down into a valley. As we were walking on that path, there was a bench on the side of the path. I went over to the bench and sat down. Jesus joined me. As we sat there together, I noticed that directly across from where we were seated there was a magnificent door. I could not see the house behind the door—I saw only the door.

I asked, "Lord, who lives there?"

He answered, "*That's not important. Come with me.*" He stood up and started walking again. I followed Him. When we arrived at the bottom of that path, there was a valley. In that valley there were many people just standing around as if they were waiting for Jesus? When they saw Jesus, they got very excited and applauded. Before I could really get a good look at the people or the valley, we were lifted up and elevated to another mountain. We went up and over the valley, as if we were on an invisible escalator. I observed the people as we passed over their heads. Their hands were reaching out to Jesus. When we got to the top of the new mountain, we stood on a very high peak. I became aware of the brilliance of Jesus. The light He radiated was blinding and overshadowed me. The people in the valley below were still looking in our direction. I knew that they could see Jesus, but my image was lost in the shadow of His light.

For weeks afterward, whenever I would go into meditation, I would find myself on that mountain peak, engulfed in the light of Jesus. After meditation, I would wonder why we were just standing there, not moving or going anywhere. One morning while walking to church, I noticed a mountain peak ahead of me, which reminded me of the peak we were standing on in the vision. In prayer, I asked God to explain the vision to me, and this is what came to me then. I realized that Jesus was taking over my life, transforming me into a lamp from which His light would shine. I understood also that there were people all around me in the world who were looking for Jesus and waiting for Jesus to come into their lives, and yet they could not seem to reach Him.

Jesus was teaching me all this through those visions, to make me aware of all those people who need Jesus in their lives. I thanked God for explaining the vision to me and asked Him to help me to become like Jesus for those people. After the meaning of that vision was made clear to me, during meditation that evening we began moving down off that mountain into another valley. At this time, I was having trouble again relating to Art. But after I had shared with Minica and gone back into meditation with questions on my mind, a new vision started to unfold. I saw myself walking with Jesus on a path leading into a tunnel. We entered the tunnel together. The tunnel was in the shape of a wing. It was as if we were entering into the breast of a huge bird! While we were in the tunnel, I could not see or hear anything. There was complete silence and darkness all around us. Yet, I was not afraid. Knowing that Jesus was there with me, I was comforted and was completely at peace in the darkness.

Every day during that period of time, whenever I went into meditation, I would find myself back in that dark place, where there was nothingness all around me. But I would come out of meditation knowing that everything was all right; God was with me, as He always is, and Jesus was at my side, comforting me with His love. One day in meditation, after three days of darkness, we finally came out of the tunnel into bright sunlight. The light was dazzling. I could hardly keep my eyes open. However, as my eyes adjusted to the light, I could see that we were entering into another valley. I came out of meditation realizing that another long, dark night had passed in my relationship with Art and that everything was going to be all right again.

The next morning, while I was reading the newspaper in our rumpus room, Art came into the room to talk to me. He was very pleasant and asked me what I was doing.

I answered, without looking at him, "I'm reading the newspaper."

He said, "I can see that. But what are you reading?"

"I'm looking for a place to rent, a room in someone's home."

Art said, "Darling, I don't want you to move out. I have been thinking about it. You don't have to move out. This is your home. There's room enough for the two of us. You can stay out here or move back into the bedroom, and I will sleep out here, if you want me to." He continued, "I'm not going to expect anything from you anymore. You can do whatever you want to do with your life. I won't get in your way."

"That's not going to work, Art. You have made promises like that to me before, and you are always sincere when you make them. But as soon as things are not going the way you think they should, you start blaming me again. I just will not live like this anymore. I want to be free to be me—to do whatever God is calling me to do, to become the person He wants me to be. I cannot be the person you think I should be."

Art said, "I know. I promise I won't get in your way anymore."

My answer to him was, "I will stay under one condition."

He asked, "Under what condition?"

I replied, "That we go for counseling again."

He said, "Okay. Whatever you say, but I don't want to go back to George."

"That's okay. We don't have to go back to George. We will find someone else."

We did find someone else to go to for counseling, and I moved back into our bedroom.   We continued in counseling for six weeks. Our relationship improved tremendously. At the end of six weeks, Art decided he did not want to go for counseling anymore, because it was too expensive. Christmas was just a few weeks away, and we could use the money for the holidays. He also said that in the New Year we would go back into counseling again, if we needed to. Reluctantly, I agreed. We had also decided that I would wait until the first of the year to look for a job, because I was definitely not going back to that stressful store. We both agreed that I should look for a different kind of job in the New Year. Thus, I put my typewriter away, because my mind was busy getting ready for Christmas and finding another job, not on writing a book.

After Christmas, my search began to find a new job. I didn't know what I was really looking for. Yet I knew that I did not want to go back into retail. A beautiful new hotel was opening up across the street from Robinsons. I thought it might be a nice place to work, for a change. I submitted my resume. While waiting to hear from the hotel, I was offered two jobs in cosmetics from different department stores. I thanked them for thinking about me, but said that I was looking for a different type of work.

In the meantime, Noelle brought a young man over to the house who was trying to get her interested in a home-based business opportunity for the whole family. We listened to him, and everything he said made a lot of sense to us. We told him that we would think about it. He told us to take our time.

"In fact," he said, "Tomorrow evening, a friend is having a meeting and some people will be there who are also interested in learning about this business. So, come join us, and bring the rest of your family with you who might also be interested in learning more about it."

The next evening, Art, Dennis, Noelle, and I went to the house meeting. We met some very interesting people there. They were all very friendly. We felt comfortable with them. As the young man was explaining how the business worked, he wrote something on the board. I looked at what he had written and saw these words: "I am the way." Those were not the actual words that the young man had written on the board—nonetheless, that's what I saw. I immediately thought, "This must be the business that the Lord wants us to do, as a family." On the way home in the car, I shared with my family what I had seen written on the board.

Art said, "You should have your eyes checked—you're seeing things again!"

We all laughed about it, as Art, Noelle, and Dennis discussed my vivid imagination. The next day our family discussed the business idea in detail, and we all agreed that it sounded like something that we would like to do together as a family. Naturally, it seemed sensible to me that I should do that instead of going back to work for someone else. As a matter of fact, we thought it was an answer to our prayers.

Art was tired of the uncertainties of his construction business. Noelle was working as a tour guide at Universal Studios. It was at Universal Studios that Noelle had met the friend who introduced her to this business opportunity. Dennis was also interested in doing it. I thought then that what I had seen written on the board, "I am the way," meant that this was what we should do as a family.

It was at this time during my visioning that I saw my family cross over the bridge and enter into that beautiful place on the other side. I thought it was a sign from God; this helped me to decide on doing that home-based business. I figured, also, that after the business got off the ground and we were making a living with it, I would have lots of time to finish this book. We all dove into the networking business, giving it our best and putting all our extra time and money into building it. We spent a lot of time together as a family working on our new business. Art, Dennis, and Noelle continued to work at their jobs in the daytime. But every evening, and on weekends, we were together, involved in some way with the new business. We had a great time as a family, working together, trying to build that business.

In our spare time we were listening to tapes about people who were successful. We met some very interesting individuals, who were doing well. They were professionals: doctors, lawyers, accountants, and others from all walks of life. These people all had something in common. They all believed in God and praised Him for everything. Some of them would tell their stories with tears in their eyes. One young man in particular made a great impact on Art, because he used to be a contractor before he got into that business. He and his wife told their story together. They related what kind of man he had been before he found God and how God had changed his life and made him successful. Now that they were making a good living, he was telling his story and hoping his message would help others also.

It was like that every time we went away on a business convention. One professional person after another would get up and share how God had changed their lives. Most of them were making a lot of money in that business. But each would tell their story of how it was God who changed their lives.

It was at this point in time that Art started going to church regularly with me, whether we were getting along or not. One day after we got home from church, I thanked him for going to church with me, because he had gone to bed the night before upset with me about something. Even so, that morning he had gotten dressed and gone to church without me even asking him if he was going. That was a first for Art. Yet, when I thanked him for going with me, he informed me that he hadn't gone to church for me!

He said, "I'm going to church for me! Not because you think that I should go."

I exclaimed, with joy and laughter in my voice, "Hallelujah! Praise the Lord! That's the only reason anyone should go to church—not to impress someone else or for any other reason, but for their own spiritual nourishment and experience."

From that day forward, Art went to church regularly with me on Sundays. Art did cross over a bridge into a new and higher place, a place of better understanding. He understood that God is not only for women, or the poor, or for men who are not very macho. Because of that business opportunity, we met people Art admired and men to whom he could relate. These men, from all walks of life, were not afraid to speak out for God.

The home business venture, however, was not for us. We worked at it diligently for a year. We had a good time, going away on weekend conventions and meeting interesting people. After a year, all our efforts did not produce enough money to support us. So in March of 1987 I had to go back to work. Yet, during that year while we were trying to build up that business—

though we were not successful in our efforts to make money with it—I did, nonetheless, make gigantic leaps in my spiritual growth, and so did Art. I truly believe there are lessons to be learned in every situation in life. As Saint Paul reminds us in Romans 8:28: *"All things work together for good, to those who love God and are called according to His purpose."*

14

My Baptism in Light

I am the light of the world
Whoever follows me will not walk in darkness
But will have the light of life.

—*John 8:12*

My journey with the Lord continued to move very rapidly. We had gone through the dark tunnel and had come out into the light. Jesus was now standing at the bottom of the hill that led us out of the tunnel. In front of Jesus there was a sparkling river. That river ran through the valley beneath the hill that we had just descended, and another hill loomed ahead of us.

I walked up to Jesus and said, "This is a lovely river, Lord."

Jesus said nothing but motioned with His hand for me to go into the river. I looked down at my clothing and holding my arms out to Him, I asked, "with all my clothes on?"

"Yes, Just as you are."

I protested, "But Lord, my clothes, they will get wet."

He replied, "That's all right. You will dry off."

With that, I dove into the river head first. As soon as I entered the river, I realized immediately that there was no water in it! I floated instead in a stream of light! It was beautiful! It was as if I were moving through space in a body of light! After a while, I came out of the river and went over to Jesus.

Laughing with Him, I said, "Lord that was a strange experience!"

He said, "Yes! I know."

As I looked at myself, I could see that my whole body was saturated with light from that river. The light clung to my clothes and skin. I shook my arms, legs, and clothing, as if shaking water from myself. But streams of light were clinging to me from head to toe. I came out of meditation then, fascinated by that vision.

The next day I went again into meditation. Jesus was walking on a hill a little ahead of me. I looked at myself. Streams of light still covered me.

I said, "Lord, when will this light disappear?"

Jesus answered, *"Don't worry about that. You will eventually absorb the light."*

My meditation ended. In meditation the next evening, the vision continued. Jesus was still walking ahead of me, as He had been in my vision the day before. Now, however, I was dragging behind Him. It was difficult for me to keep up with Jesus.

I said, "Lord! Please wait for me."

Jesus slowed down His pace until I caught up with Him; as I got closer to Jesus in the vision, I noticed something was different. I could not seem to get close to Him. In the past, I had been able to go up to Him and put my arms around Him.

The streams of light that were clinging to me were getting in the way. It was as if I were trapped in a shell of light. I looked down at myself again to see why I could not get close to Jesus. I noticed that the light was clinging to my arms, my head, and something that was on my back. Looking back, I saw what seemed to be a tail dragging behind me. I looked at Jesus and then at myself again. He and I were different from one another. He looked as He always had to me, but I was different now. The light was showing me our differences. I came out of meditation, saddened by the fact that I could not get close to Jesus. That really bothered me. I prayed about that all night, remembering what I had looked like in the vision. I could not stand the fact that I was not like Jesus. While I was praying about that, asking God to take away my ugliness, this Scripture verse came into my mind. When Jesus was speaking to His disciples about John the Baptist, He said of him, *"… among those born of women, there has been none greater than John the Baptist; yet the least in the Kingdom of Heaven is greater than he"* (Matthew 11:11). I kept thinking of that verse. It has always baffled me. I wondered why Jesus had said that about John the Baptist—*"the least in the Kingdom of Heaven is greater than he."*

As I walked to church the next morning, I remembered the vision and how different I had looked from Jesus. I recalled what Jesus had said: "The least in the Kingdom of God is greater than those born of women." I went into the church and asked God to explain the vision to me. After Mass, I continued my morning walk, still praying about that vision. As I walked, I was praying in tongues; I cried as I prayed, asking God to help me to understand the words

I was saying. My voice then became like that of a little child. Still praying in tongues, but now understanding my request as I prayed, I said:

"Father, please take away my ugliness. I don't want to be an animal in Your Kingdom! I want to be like Your Son, Jesus—to look like Him, act like Him, and love like Him. I want to be like Him in every way and to be your daughter, Father, not just to be an ugly animal in your kingdom."

As I walked and prayed, my eyes were wide open, yet my vision continued from where I had left off the day before in meditation. I saw myself walking behind Jesus, trapped in a shell of ugliness. I looked like a prehistoric animal! There were (scale-like) spikes on my head, which continued down my back and ended in a long tail. Streams of light were clinging to those scales, which kept me away from Jesus. I wanted so much to run over to Jesus and to hug Him, just as I had always done in the past. Yet I could not reach Him. Also, at this point Jesus was twice my height. I seemed to have shrunk in size. By this time I was sobbing uncontrollably. My sobs were those of a child. I prayed, still in tongues, but now I understood every word as if I were praying in English. My prayers continued, with sincerity, from the depths of my soul, to our Heavenly Father, and then to Jesus.

Jesus, still walking ahead of me, suddenly stopped, turned around, looked at me, and said, *"Come, Madelene."*

With that, I was released from my ugly shell of confinement.

Joy filled my heart. Excitedly, I began jumping up and down like a playful child, swinging my arms up, down, and turning around in one spot, laughing, as I said in a loud voice, "I'm free! I'm free! I'm free!"

With that, I ran over to Jesus. On approaching Him, I realized again that He was twice my size! I was now a little girl about the age of six. Jesus picked me up and carried me for a while. Then he put me down again. After He put me down, I playfully ran ahead of Him.

Jesus then called out to me in a firm voice: *"Madelene! Come back here! Don't get ahead of me! I don't want you to get into trouble!"*

I replied, "Yes, Lord."

I ran back to Him and took hold of His hand; we continued our walk together. This vision unfolded as I walked home from church.

That evening before dinner, I went again into meditation, and the vision continued. We had reached the top of the hill and were standing looking down into the San Fernando Valley. I realized that we were back on earth; in my neighborhood. I observed the surroundings. There was no one on that hill with us. But—my typewriter was there and the table on which I kept it! My thought was, "What's my typewriter doing here?"

With that, Jesus said, *"Sit down, Madelene."*

As Jesus said that, a chair was placed in front of me. I sat down on the chair, but could hardly reach the typewriter.

I said, "Lord, I don't know how to type."

He was standing at the left side of the typewriter in front of me and said, *"That's all right, Madelene; I will help you."*

My meditation then ended.

For many weeks after that, every time I went into meditation, Jesus and I would be on the same hill, in the same place, with me at my typewriter. I seemed to be waiting for Him to tell me what to type. Yet nothing was happening. One day I got up off the chair and was walking around that hillside. Some people on another part of the hill were all standing, looking up into the sky, singing and giving praise to God. Jesus and I were walking between and around them, but they were unaware of our presence. They totally ignored us; it was as if we were not even there.

I asked Jesus, "Who are these people, Lord, and what are they doing?"

He said, "They are looking for me up in the sky, but I'm in their midst, and they are not even aware of Me."

With that, we were back at my typewriter. Some of those people were walking around the typewriter, not even seeing it, and they almost pushed the typewriter over the hill. Jesus snapped His fingers, and a round, transparent tube came down (as if from heaven) and covered the typewriter, table, chair, Jesus, and me. It was a transparent shield that protected us from the environment and the people around us.

During that period of time, I was attending the Thursday morning prayer group at Saint Bernardine's, in my previous parish in West Hills. One morning, as we were praying and worshiping God, I looked at everyone in the prayer group. We were all sitting with our hands raised up, praying and singing in tongues. Then I remembered the people in my vision who were looking up into the sky, and what Jesus had said made me feel that I was wasting precious time. There was something inside of me that was becoming very restless. I had enjoyed the group for a year. Now, working again, my time was limited, even though my new job allowed me more freedom than any other job I had had in the past. I was able to take time off during the day to go to prayer group or do whatever I needed to do. During the time I was in that prayer group, however, I really did grow in understanding of God's love. Yet, there were people there who really needed to be touched by God's love.

One day, while driving to work after attending the prayer group meeting, I asked God to use me in whatever way He needed. I said, *"Lord, I am yours. Do with me what You will. Just tell me what You want me to do and how to do it. Show me the way to your Kingdom, Lord, and teach me how to bring others into Your Kingdom."*

While praying, I drove the freeway to Simi Valley, to one of my accounts. The Lord spoke to my heart, saying, *"Madelene, I want you to love."*

I answered, "Yes, Lord, I know, but what else do you want me to do?"

He answered again, *"Just love."*

I asked again, "But, Lord, there must be something else that I could do with my life."

The Lord said again, *"Madelene, I want you to be my disciple of love. I want you to touch others with my love."*

During the year that I was attending the prayer group, my visions were the most frequent.

Art and I had been married thirty years, and our thirty-first anniversary was approaching fast. In our first thirty years of marriage, we had never received Holy Communion, because we were not married in the Church. Art had been married before in the Catholic Church, so we were unable to receive the sacraments, according to the Church. Yet I knew people who were in the same position we were in who went to communion regularly. I felt, however, that it would be hypocritical to say that we were Catholics and not abide by the rules of the Catholic Church.

A year before our thirtieth anniversary, however, we went to our pastor of Saint Bernardine's Church to see if he could help Art obtain an annulment from his first marriage. Art had been twenty-two years old when he had married the first time. He had been overseas in the Philippines. He married a woman who was ten years his senior. She divorced him after he brought her to this country, and she married someone she had known from the Philippines. When Art and I met, he had been divorced for three years. Art's first wife did not tell him before they were married that she had a child, who lived with her mother in the country, and that she could not have any more children. Art knew nothing about any of this until after they were married.

After we had related Art's story to our pastor, he assured us that we would have no trouble getting an annulment from his first marriage. But he said that we would have to track Art's ex-wife down, because the Church would want to hear her side of the story. It took Art about six months to locate his former wife. He made the contact with her in the Philippines. Art explained to her what we were trying to accomplish and asked if she would be willing to help us. She wrote to Art saying, "Sorry, but I can't help you. Good luck on your thirtieth anniversary."

We took her letter to our pastor, showed it to him, and asked, "Now what, Father?"

He said, "Well, there's nothing the Church can do if she won't cooperate with us."

We thanked him and left his office, thinking that it didn't make any sense to us that the Church considered Art still married to his ex-wife and not to me. Nevertheless, I thought to myself that God loves us anyway, and, just because we can't receive communion, that does not mean we are not forgiven for our sins just like everyone else.

I would have continued as we were until death, because every time people in the church went to communion, I also went in spirit, receiving the Lord in my heart. It really bothered Art, though, that I was not allowed to receive communion.

One day after church at breakfast, Art said, "I can understand the Church not letting me receive communion. But," he said, "I'm sure that there is no one in that church who is any closer to God than you are, so why should you be denied communion?"

I told him, "It really makes no difference to me if I receive communion or not, because God lives in my heart, and he is always with me."

After this conversation with Art, I went into meditation that afternoon, speaking to God and asking him to heal me and make me whole. While in meditation, I saw myself sitting at the typewriter. Jesus was standing at the left side, in front of the typewriter. A stream of light was shining down from Heaven upon Him. He stood there in front of me and said, *"Madelene, I want you to think, now."*

I answered, "Yes, Lord."

He said, *"Think transformation."*

I repeated, "Think transformation."

With that, I closed my eyes in the spirit and I said it again. As if trying to understand what He was saying to me, I repeated, *"Transformation."* With my eyes still closed in the vision, I repeated again, *"Think transformation."* Then, still in meditation, I opened my "spiritual eyes" after repeating those words several times to myself. The vision continued. Now, however, Jesus was gone. Yet I was still sitting at the typewriter in the same place as I'd been before I closed my "spiritual eyes" in that vision, and I was still a little girl about the age of six.

The light was streaming down from Heaven. Jesus was gone, and I was left there, by myself, sitting in the light at the typewriter. Sadness filled my heart, as tears ran down my cheeks. I asked, with distress in my voice, "Lord, where are you? Please don't leave me, Lord!"

Then I heard His voice. I could not see Him; I heard only His voice. He said,

"I will never leave you. I am with you always, even to the end of the earth. I am the breath of your breath, the blood of your blood, the flesh of your flesh, the bone of your bones. You cannot separate yourself from me; be transformed. Know the truth, and the truth will set you free. I am in you, and you are in me. I will

never leave you. I love you with a love that is everlasting. Be transformed. Think transformation!"

The vision ended, and I came out of meditation thinking of the word, *transformation*. I repeated to myself, *"Be transformed."* Yet, sadness filled me, because at the end of that vision I could not see Jesus. My meditation ended that evening with a feeling of sadness. Yet, in spite of my disappointment over Jesus' disappearance from the vision, all that night and throughout the next day, I remembered His words to me:

"I love you with a love that is everlasting; I would never leave you. I'm with you always, even to the end of the earth.

I kept His encouraging words to me in my thoughts—they helped me to experience, throughout the night and all of the next day, the warmth of His love embracing me.

15

CALLED TO BE TRANSFORMED

Do not conform yourself to this age
But be transformed by the renewal of your mind
That you may discern what is the will of God,
What is good and pleasing and perfect!

—Romans 12:2

The next evening, as I sat in meditation with my eyes closed and remembered the vision from the day before, I said to myself, *"Think transformation."* With that, I was back again in the same place where I had left off the day before. As I sat at the typewriter, streams of light were still shining down from heaven. Jesus was gone; I was all alone, just sitting there wondering where Jesus was. After waiting for a while to see if He would return, I got up from the typewriter and walked around in the transparent tube that Jesus had placed around the typewriter and me for protection.

I looked up at the light to see from where it was coming. It was shining down through the hollow tube. As I looked up at the light, the transparent tube moved its position and leaned sideways. I began to walk inside the tube toward the top. As I walked and explored the tube, wondering what it was, the thought came to me that it was a hollow tree. My walk continued inside the body of that tree. There were branches growing outwardly in different directions; they, too, were hollow. On entering one of those branches, I continued my walk inside it for a while and then saw an opening, which I entered. That opening brought me to the outside of a gigantic tree. That tree towered over all the buildings in the area. I could see Robinsons Department Store and the new hotel across the street from Robinsons. The branch on which I now stood was on a tree that was six times the height of Robinsons or the new hotel.

I came out of meditation, fascinated by the experience—I felt like Alice in Wonderland. I knew in my heart that the Holy Spirit was teaching me through those visions and that the meaning would be made clear to me in time. The next evening, as I meditated, the vision continued. It began with me standing in the same place on the branch of that huge tree, just looking around, trying to understand why I was there and what was going to happen next. My attention was drawn to the branch on which I was standing. I noticed that it was alive with leaves and flowers. Some of the flowers were changing their form. My interest and concentration immediately shifted and focused on one flower in particular that was in the process of changing. In the center of that flower, a tiny green fruit was beginning to emerge. At that point, the vision ended.

The next morning, as I walked to church, I prayed, asking the Lord to explain the vision to me. The Holy Spirit assured me that my spirit was observing the unfolding process of change within myself—my own transformation. A slow dying of self was taking place.

That evening, in meditation, the vision again continued. I found myself standing on the same branch, observing the flower and the tiny fruit that was now visible. It was green in color but had a different shape. While focusing on that fruit, trying to analyze what kind of fruit it was, I came out of meditation.

The next morning on my way to church, while walking and praying for understanding, I wondered what kind of fruit was coming forth out of "God's mystical tree." I knew in my heart that it represented the place where I was in my spiritual growth and understood at the same time that God's Holy Spirit was about to bear fruit in me. While thinking of the vision, I remembered everything about the flowers and leaves on that mystical branch. I also recalled the smell and texture of the developing fruit, on which my senses were now focused, and it gave me the distinct impression that the green substance that was slowly emerging from the center of that mystical flower was going to be some kind of citrus fruit.

That evening, again in meditation, I was standing on that mystical branch, observing the same fruit. It had now begun to ripen. The color was slightly yellow. While I was deep in thought, analyzing the fruit, a voice said to me, *"It's a lemon!"* I looked around and saw that Jesus was again at my side on that huge, mystical tree.

I looked at Him, surprised to see Him there, as I repeated, with a question in my voice, *"A lemon, Lord?"*

He answered, *"Yes! That fruit is a lemon."*

I came out of meditation with disappointment in my heart, thinking, *"I'm a lemon?"*

I called my friend, Minica Bond, to share the vision with her. After sharing everything about the vision up to that point, I said, with disappointment in my voice, "So, Minica, I'm a lemon!"

We laughed about it. Then Minica said, "But Madelene, lemons adds flavor to food, and it makes a refreshing drink!"

The next morning on my walk to church, I remembered what Minica had said about the purpose of lemons. I prayed about it, and the Lord spoke to my heart. He said,

"Madelene, you are a refreshing drink to those who are thirsty, and you will give flavor to my words. There are so many people who do not understand me and the purpose of my coming into the world. Be my light, Madelene. Let them see my love shining through you."

That evening in meditation, I was still a little girl, standing on the huge tree, looking down at the city beneath me. Jesus was at my side. He took hold of my hand and said, *"Come."* We walked off the tree onto a road. On that road there was someone waiting for us. Jesus said, *"Madelene, this is my Father."*

With that, I said, "Lord! I want Art to meet Him too!"

As I said that, Art was there with us. He was also a little child. I took hold of Art's hand, as we started to walk on that road. We walked for a little while. Jesus was with us, but God the Father had vanished from the vision. God the Father had been there only for a moment, as we stepped onto that road. Now Art was in the scene, and Jesus was with us, as we walked together. After a while, Jesus picked Art up and carried him in His arms. Art seemed to be sound asleep in the arms of Jesus. Art was about the size of a two-year-old. Through meditation, Jesus walked with me on that road for months. Art was always with us. Jesus showed me many things while I walked with Him. But, like a little two-year-old, Art would get tired of walking and Jesus would carry Him while he slept.

One day in meditation, the vision changed. Jesus, Art, and I came to some very wide steps. As we walked up those steps, Jesus was in the middle. He held Art's right hand and my left, as the three of us walked together up to the top of those steps. When we got to the top, there was a very large table. The table was completely covered with a white cloth, which hung to the floor. I could not see what was on top of the table, because I was too short. Neither could I see under the table or around it. I stood there for a moment. Then Jesus let go of Art's hand, bent over, picked me up with both of His hands around my waist, and sat me on the table. I looked at Jesus and then at the table.

On the table there was a huge cross, which completely covered its length. Jesus was on the cross. I looked at the cross and then at Jesus, wondering, "How could He be in two places at the same time?" With that thought, my eyes focused on Jesus again, and He said to me, *"Eat,"* as He pointed to the cross with His hand. As I looked back at the cross on the table, I saw Jesus' body crumbling off the cross to become pieces of meat that filled up a platter on the table—and the platter of meat was placed in front of me. I then began eating what seemed to be the meat of Jesus' flesh. I ate all that I could of that platter of meat, until I was full to capacity. When I was through eating, the platter was half empty. I looked at Jesus, who was just standing there watching me eat until I was satisfied.

Jesus then lifted me off the table and put me back on the floor, next to Art. Jesus took hold of our hands again and walked us around behind the table. As we walked around that table, we came to some more steps. There was a huge throne-chair in the middle of the first step. Sitting on that chair was our Heavenly Father! Jesus presented us to His Father. Art and I knelt down in front of our Father. As we were kneeling there, I began to grow, getting taller and bigger than Art. I was the size of an adult again, but Art, kneeling next to me, was still a little boy. I stood up then, realizing at that moment that I had developed wings. I looked back at my wings and came out of meditation.

That event in meditation happened the last week of Lent, in 1986. Good Friday evening of that same week, Saint Bernardine's Church had a special evening of meditation on the crucifixion of Jesus. That evening at this special session commemorating the death of Jesus Christ, the guest priest for the evening led us into prayerful meditation. While we were in meditation, my vision continued. I saw myself kneeling in front of our Heavenly Father. I seemed to be in a distant place, far away from everyone. While I was kneeling there, two angels appeared, one on each side of me. Our Heavenly Father motioned to them to pick me up. The angels picked me up from my knees. Standing up, I realized that my hands were tied behind my back. The angels then untied my hands and my wings. Our Heavenly Father motioned with His hand to take me. The two angels picked me up and carried me by my wings: over hills, meadows, and a mountain, back down into another valley. They placed me on a lower hill below the mountain over which we had just flown. While they were carrying me, I wondered why I was not allowed to fly on my own power.

After the angels placed me on the hill, I could see people just standing around in the valley beneath us. I was dressed in a long, white robe. My wings had vanished. There was a shepherd's staff in my right hand, and on my head there was something that looked like a bishop's cone-shaped hat. My attention shifted to the people who were just standing around in the valley. To the right of where I was standing, there was a path leading down to the valley, from where the two angels had just brought me. I motioned to the people who were looking at me as if they were waiting for my instructions. I pointed to the path with the staff that was in my right hand. Seeing the staff, they began to walk up the hill and then onto the path where I was directing them. The vision ended. I came out of meditation with a feeling of true bliss. I believed in my heart that our Heavenly Father had commissioned me to point the way to His Kingdom to all who might have lost sight of Jesus.

I Am a Lemon!

You guided me through the darkness.
Therefore, now that I have reached my fullness
I give back to you the very substance of my being.
Take what I am, and use me
So that my destiny will be fulfilled,
For the lemon that I am has ripened with age.
It's time to give back to the earth
The seed of my fruit
So that more can be produced
From the core of my shell
To flavor and refresh, as lemons do so well.
Hence, as I am now picked, sliced, and squeezed
No screech will be heard from the pain
Since that is the reason, and purpose, for which I came!

16

CALL TO OBEDIENCE

If you love me,
You will keep my commandments.
And I will ask the Father
And he will give you another Advocate
To be with you always

—John 14:15–16

Easter Sunday, 1997! It's been almost nine years since my call from the Lord to document the events of my life. All of the foregoing chapters were put together in 1988. In the epilogue, I will explain the reasons for the delay. All the chapters after this one were also compiled in 1988.

In Holy Week of 1997 I took a six-day break from work so that the editing of this book would be completed. Yet, as of this date, it is in no way near completion. My lack of literary skills is still getting in the way of my progress. Art, and others, are wondering why it's taking me so long to complete the editing. The writing and editing of this book have been extremely difficult for me, with all the interfering circumstances in my life. Since I began the process of the editing in December 1996, every time I stop working on it, thinking that it's just a foolish dream, I'm pushed into submission again by the prompting of the Holy Spirit.

In the same way, the Holy Spirit was persistent with me, as He awakened me one day in the summer of 1986 at 4:00 am. This was a few months after those visions I described in the previous chapter, where Art and I were led by Jesus to that huge table, and Jesus ordered me to eat the meat of His flesh. On that summer morning, I was in bed, sound asleep. Suddenly, a deep voice awakened me, saying: *"Read Galatians."* My eyes popped open. Looking around our bedroom and seeing no one, I closed my eyes again, trying to get back to sleep. The voice repeated the words, *"Read Galatians!"* My eyes opened again. This time I looked at the clock and realized that it was only 4:00 am. Since I did not have to be at work that day until 10:00 am, I wanted to sleep a little longer.

I stayed in bed for a few moments, wondering who had spoken. I was thinking to myself that it was too early to get out of bed. Then the Holy Spirit spoke to my heart, saying, *"Madelene, get out of bed, now! And read Galatians!"* With that, I said, *"Okay, Lord! I got the message!"* Everyone was still asleep in the house. I went directly into the kitchen, plugged in the coffeepot, picked up my Bible, and began to read Galatians. I was fascinated by what I was learning, as the Holy Spirit interpreted the meaning for me. With pencil and paper in hand, I began to take notes. Throughout the rest of that day, all that I had read kept going around in my head. For about a week after that event, first thing each morning, I would read Galatians before leaving for my walk to church.

After reading Galatians every day for over a week, I went back to our priest to share with him all that I had seen through my visions and tell him about the voice that had awakened me and commanded me to read Galatians. I also shared with him my feelings about what I believed the Lord wanted me to do with His instructions though the visions, and the teachings in Galatians.

I said: "So, Father, on our next wedding anniversary, Art and I will accept the Lord's invitation to eat at His table."

Our priest then said, "You can't go to communion! Art did not get an annulment from his first marriage." And he added, "We can't live our lives by visions and dreams! This is the real world in which we live. And the Church says that Art is still married to his first wife."

I said to our pastor, "Father, are you going to sit there and tell me that you still consider Art's first wife to be his real wife, after all that you know about the situation?" I continued, "That woman left him after she got to the states and married her old sweetheart. On the other hand," I said, "We have three grown children. And I have been with Art going on thirty-one years."

He then asked me, "What will you say to your friends when they ask about you and Art receiving Holy Communion now?"

"If anyone asks, I will tell them that our problem has been resolved."

He said, "But it has not been resolved!"

My answer to him was, "To me it has." I kissed him then, said good-bye, and asked him to please pray for us.

He said, with sarcasm in his voice, "I certainly will! You and Art are going to need it."

On arriving home, I shared with Art all that transpired in meeting with our pastor. Art was disappointed to hear that Father Smith (Smith is not his real name) did not have a change of heart in our favor. I asked Art then if he would like to go to the Serra Retreat Center for our Anniversary weekend. He said," whatever you want to do is okay with me."

I called the Serra Retreat Center in Malibu, California, to find out if it was possible to attend a marriage retreat there on a weekend close to the date of our thirty-first anniversary. The lady on the phone told me that there *was* going to be a marriage retreat on our anniversary weekend, but they were already booked to capacity. I was so disappointed. I asked her to please take my name and telephone number and begged her to please let us know if anyone cancelled. She said that she would, and she added, "If it's in the will of God, you will be here that weekend." Six weeks later, we received a call from Serra Retreat Center. Thus, on our thirty first wedding anniversary, we were at the marriage retreat in Malibu.

Saturday morning of that weekend, we made an appointment to see the priest who was conducting the retreat. We related all that had transpired with our pastor, and I told him about my visions and about reading Galatians; then I added, "So, Father, this evening at Mass, Art and I will be receiving Holy Communion."

He looked at me and asked, "Why are you telling me all this?" He added, "You could have gone to communion and I would not have known the difference.

I answered him, saying, "Yes, we know that, but we have nothing to hide and wanted you to know where we are coming from."

He said in reply, "Your minds are made up, and I can see that you have reached a level of understanding in your spiritual growth that has brought you to this decision." Then he added, "You have waited all these years without receiving Holy Communion. Don't go to communion tonight; wait until tomorrow at the closing, and I will bless your marriage then."

That Sunday, November 23, 1986, we renewed our wedding vows. The priest blessed our marriage, and we received Holy Communion for the first time in thirty-one years. Before we left for home, we had an opportunity to speak to the priest again. He blessed us and told us to go in peace. He encouraged us to continue to grow in understanding of God's unconditional love for us and all people.

He also added, "Now, don't go and tell your pastor that I blessed your marriage and gave you Holy Communion!" He continued, "I get into enough trouble on my own with the bishop." He also said, "Your pastor can refuse to give you communion if he chooses; that is his right, according to the laws of the Church." He continued, "Go to another priest, or another church, to receive communion from now on, to avoid any confrontation with your pastor."

Art and I thanked him for his loving advice to us, and then we left for home.

In 1986, we were still living in our home in West Hills, in the San Fernando Valley. Walking and attending Mass each day has always been an important part of my life. Saint Bernardine's Church was one and a half miles away from our home. To find another church to go to would eliminate my time for walking, because I would have to drive to any other church nearby. Consequently, I wrote the following letter to our pastor, hoping that the "spirit of love" would help him to understand why we were so convinced that Jesus wanted us to receive communion after so many years. Smith is not his real name. His name has been changed here to protect his identity and privacy.

December 3, 1986

Dear Father Smith,

It's in the spirit of love that we write to you. Our hope is that this letter will help you to understand why, after thirty-one years of marriage, Art and I have decided to accept Our Lord's invitation to eat at His table.

Paul tells us in Galatians that God has sent the Spirit of His own Son into our hearts, so that we can rightly speak of God as our own Father. Thus, Art and I know now that the Spirit of God is living and working in us. And we believe, as Paul did, that Christ made us free—not laws and ceremonies—and that Christ is useless to us if we count on clearing our debt to God by keeping laws. All we need is faith working through love.

Now that we understand what God's law is, we know that we no longer have to force ourselves to obey church laws. "For God is love." Therefore, as long as we live in Him, as He is in us, we will always be obedient to His law, the law of love. Art and I are not looking for honors or popularity. We know that we have many faults. However, by going to communion, we are not hurting anyone or breaking any of God's laws of love.

Furthermore, after thirty-one years of repentance and feelings of unworthiness, we have come to a better understanding of God's unconditional love. Art and I know we are sinners, and we are still not worthy to receive

Him. But who is worthy? Jesus died on the cross for all sinners, not for just a few. We are forgiven our sins not by obedience to laws, but because of God's love for us—His *unconditional* love.

Our faith in Jesus Christ has freed us. We follow Him, because He has touched our hearts. Because we have been following Him, we now live in His Kingdom. We have claimed our inheritance and show our gratitude by allowing the spirit of love to guide us in every aspect of our lives. Jesus said: "Know the truth and the truth will set you free." Thank God! We are *free* at last; the chains of sin will no longer bind us to the pew in any church. Jesus paid the price for our sins when He died on the cross, so now we are free to go to Him in acceptance of His love. We say "Amen" in acknowledgment of our belief in Him and all that He has done for us—and continues to do in the life of every believer.

Because we love and respect you, Father Smith, we feel a definite obligation to clarify ourselves to you. We pray that you will understand that we are following the direction of God's Holy Spirit. Our purpose in life is to please God. Our decision was made for that reason only. Please pray for us, so that we may always live in God's pure love.

May the love of our Lord, Jesus Christ, flood your heart, so that His love will always flow from you into the lives of everyone in Saint Bernardine's Parish!

We mailed that letter in the first week of December. However, Father Smith never responded in any way to our letter. On our return from our weekend marriage retreat, we continued to go to Mass every Sunday at Saint Bernardine's, and we received communion, but always from someone else. At first, I did go to another church five miles away during the week, but after two weeks I began to walk again and attended the 8:00 am daily Mass at Saint Bernadine's. There was another priest who would say that Mass every day, so I felt safe going to Mass and communion at that time. Also, there was only a small group of people attending Mass at that hour, because the church was being remodeled. Therefore, the daily services, at 6:00 am and 8:00 am were held in one of the school classrooms. This continued until the church remodeling was completed.

One morning, in that small schoolroom, the other priest was not there because of an illness. Father Smith showed up to do the Mass. I was very uneasy throughout the service. Because of the closeness of every one in that room, there was no place for me to escape. When it was time for communion, my intent was to stay in my seat and not to go to communion that morning. Nevertheless, as I made that decision, the Lord spoke to my heart and said, *"Don't turn away from me now, Madelene. I am with you all the way."* With that, I got out of my seat and into the communion line, not knowing what was going to happen next. When I got to Father Smith, he handed me the Host and said, "The Body of Christ." I answered, "Amen," as I received Holy Communion from him.

We continued to attend church at Saint Bernardine's for another four years, until we moved from West Hills, in 1990, to our new home in Palm Desert, California. In the four years following that memorable morning, I had dealings with Father Smith many times, because I was an active member of Saint Bernardine's Parish. Father Smith was always pleasant to me, but he never acknowledged my letter to him.

Originally it was not my intent to relate any of this. Nor is it my purpose now to give the impression that anyone can do whatever they feel like doing and not follow Church rules. Art and I lived by the rules of the Catholic Church for thirty-one years. And the Catholic Church continued to be my place of worship. (Art is now worshiping the Lord in his heavenly home.) I'm an active member of Sacred Heart Church in Palm Desert, and I have become more involved in church ministries since Art's passing.

I have related these awesome experiences because of the prompting of God's Holy Spirit. *Please read Galatians*—so that you may better understand the meaning of my letter to the pastor at Saint Bernardine's Church in Woodland Hills, California.

17

My Commission

I came into the world as light
So that everyone who believes in me
Might not remain in darkness

—*John 12:46*

For months I continued to go regularly to the Saint Bernardine's prayer group. However, after the visions described in chapter 15, I became very restless. Believing that the Lord had commissioned me to help His lost people find their way back to Him, I shared all that the Lord was teaching me about His love with the prayer group. I sensed that they were getting a little tired of me talking so much about God's love. Some in that group seemed to talk more about the devil and his powers than the power of God's love!

One morning, while reading Scriptures and meditating; I stopped to pray for everyone in the prayer group, asking God to fill us with His love and wisdom. While I was praying, the Lord spoke to my heart and said: "Madelene, write this down." Immediately, I began to write on an empty page in my Bible. This is what I wrote on February 9, 1987.

> Today the Holy Spirit revealed to me that we who are Christians have nothing to fear but fear it- self because Jesus died to destroy the power of sin over us. We must not fall away from faith in Him. When we do, we lose sight of Him and will slip back into darkness. When we walk in darkness, we walk in fear—fear controls us, and we lose sight of God. There is no darkness in God. Thus, when we live in Him, His light protects us and will keep us from all evil. When we know the truth, the truth will set us free. The truth is:

"God is Love." And because He is love, we have *nothing* to fear from our beloved creator and Father. When we live in His love, love becomes a living, breathing, thinking part of us. Then!—we are transformed by that love to become lamps from which His light shines. Furthermore, the truth will rule our lives. We will lose all fear of Satan and will destroy Satan's image as a god over us. All honor, glory, and praise will go to God and God alone. God, as a loving Father, will correct His children whenever we need to be corrected. Yet, some of us are walking in God's light with blindfolds over our eyes, because we are afraid of what we might see. God wants us to remove the blindfolds, so that we can grow in the spirit of love and understanding for each other and all people. Jesus wants to take us into His Father's Kingdom, but we must first be transformed by His love. We are all God's children, and God loves each and every one of us in the very same way. His love does not depend on our goodness. Good or bad, we are all loved unconditionally. However, when we understand what God's love is and we accept His love unconditionally, we will be blessed by the power of His Holy Spirit. The Spirit of God will live in us and will work through us, so the world will know that we are all one in Him, because we love. By the fruit of love we shall be known. Then every Christian can truly say, as Saint Paul did: I live no more, for now Christ lives in me. (Galatians 2:20)

After I was through writing, the Lord again spoke and said, *"Share this message with the prayer group."* The message was well received by many, but a few were upset with that message. I continued to attend the prayer group, sharing whatever the Lord wanted me to share with them, as I share with you now. We cannot live in a daze and be oblivious to the truth. There is evil all around us. But, the truth is, we will never destroy evil with evil. Love overcomes evil. The power of love is stronger than all the powers of hell! Consequently, we, as Christians, are called to become lamps from which the love of Christ will shine. Light penetrates darkness. The opposite of love is sin. Those who sin live in darkness and are starving for love.

We have got to stop giving so much power to the devil! Jesus crushed the devil's deceiving head when He died on the cross. The darkness of death did not keep Christ in a tomb. Jesus rose victoriously on Easter Sunday. We who believe in Jesus must also be raised with Him into the transforming light of

God's love. Everything in God's Holy Book points to the power of His love. His love is the shield that protects us from the evil powers of darkness. The opposite of darkness is light. We are all called to be the light of Christ in the world, to triumph over evil. Yes! Let's remove the blindfolds from our eyes and stop blaming others for all the problems that exist in the world today. We must be responsive to the needs of others. Let's stop expecting others to make things right for us. Let's stand together as one body in Christ, strong in the power of God's love and forgiveness. Let's put the devil in his place! He has no power over us when we follow Jesus and live in God's Kingdom. Let's live in God's Kingdom now—here on this earth!

Let's not wait until we die to get acquainted with Jesus. Let's invite Jesus into our lives now, so that He can be the light of our righteousness. Let's be transformed! Let's put on the mind of Christ. Let us truly surrender ourselves to God's Holy Spirit, so that Christ may, indeed, live in us. Let's use the power of God's love to attract others into His light. Let us become radiant with God's love to deplete the darkness in the world. Let's not judge others for all the wrong things they do. Let's remove the beam from our own eyes, before we try to help others to remove the splinter from theirs (Matthew 7:3).

Let's stop thinking that we must defend God. Let God defend us! Let's put on the shield of His righteousness. Jesus is God's righteousness. Let's become Jesus to the world. No one can destroy the power of God's love! Jesus showed us the power of His love when He died on the cross! He gave His life for us so that we could understand how much God loves us. Paul tells us (in I Corinthians 13) that love is the only thing that lasts forever.

The poem "I'm Free" was written at Christmas season of 1986. I wrote this poem after experiencing the vision of eating the meat of Jesus' flesh and having my wings untied.

Christmas 1986

Madelene's Revelation

The Word became flesh and dwelt among us.
The Word is truth, and truth will free us.
The Word is light, and light gives life to us.
The Word is love, and love will shine from us.
I'm free! I'm free! I'm free!
I'm out of the darkness now; everyone can see:
The light of Christ has transformed me.
Now my life is filled with love that glows
Like an enchanting river, its beauty flows
Into the lives of everyone I meet
To start a fire in their souls,
As our hearts together beat.
I count my blessings as I go,
Giving praise to the Lord for what I know;
My wings of freedom have been untied.
Now I move with the wind beneath the sky,
Inviting everyone to come with me
Into the light that has made me free!

18

CHRIST IS OUR ROBE OF RIGHTEOUSNESS

There is no salvation through anyone else
Nor is there any other name under heaven
Given to the human race by which we may be saved.

—*Acts 4:12*

If all who believe themselves to be Christians become fully acquainted with Jesus, they will then completely comprehend the reason why He died on the cross. And all will be raised with Him into His glorious light of understanding. Christians need to understand that we are fighting a losing battle as long as we continue to think that we have all the answers or we don't need God or anyone else—or we can make it on our own. Since the world began, humanity has been thinking that way. God sent prophets to help us understand our wrong thinking and to point the way to peace and happiness.

We have been told through the ages that money and power without God lead only to selfishness and destruction. Even so, we do not listen to God's prophets. Instead, we kill and destroy for more power and money, keeping ourselves in bondage to the sin of wrong thinking. God, seeing our blindness, came into our midst as one of us to show us the way to overcome our selfishness. He emptied Himself of His divinity, so that He could be as we are, in all things except sin. Jesus' purpose for coming into the world was to show us the way back into our Heavenly Father's Kingdom. *However, if we turn our backs on Jesus, He cannot help us!* Those of us who believe in Jesus must understand that the only way that we will ever help our lost brothers and sisters to find their way back to God is to allow the risen Christ to love them through us.

The world will never become what God intended it to be if we keep moving farther away from God and deeper into darkness. We who are Christians must become shining examples to those who don't know Christ. We must put on "His robe of righteousness"—but not be condemning of others or acting as if we have it all. We don't have it all! We don't have all the answers! God alone has the answers.

When we want to know what God thinks about anything, we must ask Jesus. He came into the world with all the answers, to show us how to behave and act toward each other. When we become like Jesus to the rest of the world, we will attract others into His light. Christ then, will become for us our robe of righteousness.

Unfortunately, some of us who call ourselves Christians have failed miserably! How can we ever begin to teach a sinful world about God's love and His goodness when, by our actions, we tell others that we don't really believe it ourselves? We are so afraid of the devil and the powers of hell. We look for Satan everywhere we go, and we give him credit for everything that goes wrong in our lives! Why do the people of God give so much power to Satan? Don't we believe in Jesus? Why did Jesus die on the cross? Was He crazy? Did Jesus do all that just for attention? These are questions we must keep asking ourselves until we find the answers. The answer, as I see it, dear brothers and sisters, is love. Love makes all things right. We are told to love one another. When we show love, the world will know that we are one with Christ. Love is infectious. It will spread like a purifying fire, burning away the darkness of our souls, attracting others to its warmth and beauty.

There is no resistance to love. Everything in the universe has a need to be loved and to love. The creator of the universe, who *is* love, has placed Himself in the center of His creation. He can never leave us, because He is in us. But we have turned our focus from Him! God wants our full attention, so that He can draw forth that part of Himself that's within us. We will never be satisfied, until we get in touch with that part of ourselves. The problem is that as long as we are traveling in the opposite direction from where God is, we will never find Him. That's why it became necessary for Jesus to come into the world and to die for us. He told us, through His death, that not even death can separate us from the love of God when we believe in Him and trust in Him. Let us put our trust and faith in Jesus, so that He can do a new thing in us. Then, He will transform us. So let's "put on the mind of Christ."

Let's die to our old ways of thinking. Let's nail ourselves to the cross with Jesus and die to everything that is not of Him. Look at Jesus hanging on the cross. God did not put Him there. *We* did, because we refused to believe the word of God. God raised Jesus up into His glorious light of salvation, so we, God's lost children, could find our way back into His beautiful garden of bliss. Let truth be our guide to freedom.

Jesus Christ is the truth of God. When we open our eyes to Jesus, we will see God. He and the Father are one! Because Jesus died for us, we now have the power of God's Holy Spirit living in us. God's Holy Spirit is alive and well! Let's surrender ourselves to God's Holy Spirit, so that He can bear fruit in us. The fruit of God's Holy Spirit is love. Let's give birth to love. Then, the world will come to know that, God is love, and in Him there is no darkness..

My Feelings of Love!

When I think of love, I think of God.
We cannot separate God from love, or love from God.
Love is the life-giving substance of every human soul.
When we love, we bear fruit to God, in the world.
So, this love that I bring, it's not a fleeting thing
It's love Himself, who loves through me.
Before love held me, I was nothing
But now that I have embraced love, Love is everything!
The immortal spirit of love is Lord of my soul
The warmth that radiates from Him never grows cold.
Love is the light that brightens each day.
Love shines forth to show us His way.
Without love, life is sad to live
But when we love, life to love we give.
To infuse love is my greatest desire.
A spark from love can set the world on fire.
And as love ignites in everyone's heart
It will purify each soul, to make each a part
Of one Holy Spirit, as we were all meant to be
United through love for all eternity.
This love of which I speak, it's not ours to keep.
love cannot be restrained, it will flow like rain
For, life it must sustain.
Love makes all things new; love is the producer of life
And through life, love is ours to share.
When we reach out to love
Love will capture us and transform us
And will make us all a part of His enormous heart.
When we love, anger is defused, self-pity is buried,
Resentment loses its sting, and hurts are quickly healed.
Love defends all that is good.
Love gives courage to those who are meek.
Love is always forgiving—never demanding.
Love is gentle and courteous—never rude.
Love is understanding and is sensitive to the needs of others.
Love is the seed of life, love makes all things right;
Hence, when we love, we bring forth God's light
Because "God is Love, and in Him there is no darkness."
So, let us pray that people everywhere

Will enter into the light of love.
Then! The world will see God as Father,
And will know that we are all His children.
Because we love!

Let's read again 1 Corinthians 13, Saint Paul's beautiful lesson on love.

19

A NEW REVELATION

He reveals profound mysteries beyond man's understanding
He knows all hidden things, for He is light,
And darkness is no obstacle to Him

—Daniel 2:22

The following chapter, "A Note to the Readers" was completed before this one; I intended it to be the last chapter in this book. However, the following Sunday in church, while kneeling next to Art, as everyone was singing and praising God, I was elevated to a higher place in the spirit. This is what I saw in my mind's eye. As the priest lifted the Host, I closed my eyes to pray, and my spirit ascended into another location just above the church. As the vision began, I saw myself holding Art's hand as we walked together up to the altar, and then beyond, through the top of the church, as if there were an opening above the altar and invisible steps which led us to that spiritual place.

When we got to the top of the steps, we stepped off onto a transparent veil that extended beyond us and into the vastness of space. As we entered that place, our Heavenly Father was sitting in a huge chair in front of us. Art and I were little children again; we knelt before the Father, worshipping Him. I could hear everyone in the church singing, "Lamb of God, who takes away the sins of the world, have mercy on us."

With that prayer, my attention shifted from the Father to Jesus, who was sitting on the right side of the Father, in His own chair. Art and I got up and walked over to Jesus and knelt in front of Him. In prayer, I thanked Jesus for all that He had done for us and is still doing for everyone who believes in Him. I found myself aware of everyone who was praying and praising God in all the churches throughout the world. Still in prayer, I asked Jesus to make him-self available to them and to enter into the hearts of all people, so that everyone might experience the joy of God's love. As I was praying, Jesus got up from where He was seated and took hold of my hand. I was still a little child. Jesus and I walked together into a circle. I was aware that we were in a special place just above the church. I could see everyone in the church and could hear all the voices of God's people from all over the world, giving praise to God. The sound of their praises filled my heart with joy.

Looking down into the church, I saw that the top of the church was open, and the church became a round sort of spacecraft, just floating in space. The veil-like substance on which Jesus and I were standing was also supporting that huge round bowl-like vessel as it floated in space. That vessel had no top. It was as though the earth was cut in half, the top half removed, and the bottom half scooped out to accommodate all of God's people who were singing praises to Him.

After walking away from where we had left Art, Jesus and I came to a place about halfway around the huge circle. As we stopped walking and stood still, I looked down at the people in the church below us, then at a light that was shining from heaven down on us. I looked at Jesus again. He was still holding me by the hand. The light that was shining down on us had the colors of a rainbow. We stepped on the rainbow; it was solid. We moved upward in the direction of the light. We moved rapidly, ascending into the light. The closer we came to the source of the light, the brighter it became, and the louder the praises of God's people became.

We entered into a place where there were people everywhere, singing and praising God. God the Father was there, sitting on a chair in the center of all the people. We seemed to be in an enclosed area. Jesus fell on His knees in worship of the Father, and I knelt on the right side of Jesus in front of the Father.

As Jesus was kneeling there, I pulled on the sleeve of His garment to get His attention. Looking up at Jesus, as a child would, I asked: *"Lord, where are we?"*

Jesus answered, *"We are in the throne room of the Father."*

I said in reply, "But, Lord, I thought we had to die before we would come here."

In answer, Jesus said, *"Madelene, this is the place of awareness, a place of understanding, where all of God's people come when they have been enlightened. It's a place of endless love, a place where all voices join together in unity of love."*

As Jesus said these words to me, I could again hear the voices of God's people singing from the earth, in beautiful harmony, the praises of God's love. I looked back down to the earth through the rainbow-colored rays of light that descended from where we were. I noticed the light was in the shape of an

131

S. The center of the *S* touched the place where Art was still kneeling, where Jesus and I had left him.

The rays from that light continued down to the people in the bowl-like vessels and beyond, through the earth, into space. I looked up and observed that the rainbow-colored rays from that light also extended in the other direction over our heads and into the Heavens above. The rays from that light continued in both directions. I also realized then that we were in an area that was protected by a transparent substance, very much like the substance of that tube that Jesus had placed over me and my typewriter on the hillside back on earth. As I came to that realization, I found myself back again at the base of that huge tree—the one on which I had been standing when Jesus said, "It's a lemon," referring to me. I realized then that the transparent substance which formed a protective shield around me and my typewriter was everywhere in space and all around the earth. That transparent substance, I believe, is the invisible presence of God, which holds everything together throughout the universe. It's also the breath of God, which sustains the life within us and in all living things.

I would like to share with you now a poem I wrote twenty-five years earlier, entitled: "Thank You, God." This poem was written shortly after I had my "born-again" experience. After Jesus appeared to me, He changed my negative way of thinking and transformed my heart so that I could experience God within myself and see His face in the beauty of nature.

Thank You, God!

Thank You, God, for the sky so blue
For the ocean; the rain, and for the flowers, too.
Thank You for the miracle of spring
That gives life each year a new beginning.
Thank You for my rebirth
And for the beauty that surrounds us on this earth.
Thank You for the love in my heart
And for all that You, have made, of which I'm a part.
Thank You for the warmth I feel
And for the truth that You have revealed.
Thank You for Your light each day
That helps me to see my imperfect way.
Thank You for bringing me through
The darkness of night and guiding me to
This Heavenly path that leads to You!

Brothers and sisters, God, our Heavenly Father, has placed His Holy Spirit in our midst, as a shield of protection. Through His spirit of love, we can be transported into His heavenly presence. The only path to God is through love. There is no other way to find God. So let's follow the teachings of Jesus. He teaches us in Matthew 5 all that we need to know, through the *"Beatitudes*—how to be blessed and to have a purposeful life

Let's release all the hurts we are clinging to that are keeping us in bondage, and let us forgive everyone who has caused us pain. Let Jesus renew our hearts as only He can, so that we may be free in the spirit to fly into the bosom of God, where we will be embraced and nourished by Him—God, who is everywhere and is in everything—the God of love, the God of truth, the God of life. He is calling everyone back into His presence, where we, as His children, can live with Him in a state of harmony and peace in His magnificent garden of tranquility. A place of endless beauty, where there is no darkness. All who live there have become a part of God's glorious light. And they, through love, reflect His radiant beauty.

A Vision of Hope
Through the window of my mind I see
God's beautiful land of eternity,
A place where all will someday dwell
Who have conquered life and mastered it well.
As I sit each day to meditate
I drift into a blissful state,
Where God becomes the living part
Of the love that dwells within each heart.
In this place I see God's light
And with His guidance I ascend my flight,
Over the hills and meadows we go
Over the mountains to the lake below.
There with Him I rest a while
Knowing that my soul will never die,
Wishing that everyone on earth could see
This magnificent place of tranquility!

20

A NOTE TO READERS

The Spirit of the Lord is upon me
Because he has anointed me to bring glad tidings to the poor

—Luke 4:18

Dear brothers and sisters, turtle though I am, my journey with you through the pages of this book has finally come to an end. There are many more visions and learning experiences in my life that I could share with you, but I have related only those which I felt might be of some help, as you continue your own spiritual journey through life's experiences. I bid you farewell as we part. Nevertheless, my prayers will be with you, from this day forward, until the end of my life. I will be praying that God will bless all His children, wherever they may be, and that the light of His love will shine in your life to bring you safely back into His beautiful garden of bliss within yourself.

Madelene's Prayer!

Father of the homeless and of people everywhere!
Make each life a living prayer.
Let all your children learn to share
The love that's deep within each heart, which you have placed there from the
start.
Let your light be what we see; not just our own struggles and misery.
Help us not to be so slow in learning all we need to know.
Please be our wisdom in every way, as we work and when we play
Directing everyone to You by what we say and what we do.
Father, let this moment in history be, a time when everyone will see
The light that shines so very bright was sent to earth to make things right.

Let not this precious season pass; let the love that flows now forever last.
Let Your Son be born anew in the hearts of all people, not just a few.
Bring us all to Jesus now; with bending knees, to Him we'll bow.
He came to earth with love to share, to prove to us how much You care.
Forgive us, Father, for all we do that is of selfishness, but not of you.
Remove all sadness from the earth, so we may truly celebrate Your Son's birth.
Father, please bring us into Thy perfect light, so darkness will then take its
flight.
So that we will live in peace with You, knowing that Your love is true.
Please keep love's fire burning bright; let it not die in the cold of night;
Transform our minds so that we may know
It's only through love that we can grow
Into all that we are called to be
Perfect as Jesus is to Thee.
Help us then to be the Christ, to show the world
Thy perfect light

As children of God, let's take time each day to pray and meditate on His Word. Let's ask the Holy Spirit to fill our hearts with God's love and let His love be our guide in all areas of life. Let's not become brainwashed by what we see and hear on the daily news, on TV, and everywhere. Let's ask ourselves, "Is this of love?" If it is not of love, it's not of Him. Let's invite Jesus to enter our lives and allow Him be our guide. Let's not be deceived by those who might call themselves Christians yet spend more time putting others down than teaching the good news of God's love; they are not shining examples of how we should be as Christians. They are not of the light. We will see and know who is in the light, when we keep our eyes on Jesus.

As we follow Jesus, He will lead us to God, our heavenly Father. God's "Kingdom" is hidden deep within ourselves, but it can only be found when we are guided by the light of Christ.

God is the creator of all, and He is the Father of all. However, not all have as yet entered into His purifying light. Some are still struggling to find the way out of their own darkness.

We are all God's children, whether we believe in Him or not. There's not a person on this earth who is not a child of God, and His love and forgiveness for each of us is without conditions and within our reach—there is nothing that we have ever done or ever *can* do that will change His love for us. The only difference is that some of our brothers and sisters in this world do not yet understand how much God loves them! They have never experienced unconditional love in any shape or form. Thus, they believe that God is beyond their reach. That's a lie from the voice of darkness.

Let's push away darkness from the face of the earth by becoming the light of truth in the world. Let's not condemn those who do not understand the message of God. Let's love them into understanding! Let's be the Christ that everyone can see, so that all of God's children, wherever they may be, might come to know God through us. Let's show Jesus to the world.

Those whose lives bear fruit to the good news of God's unconditional love are walking with Jesus; He is in them, and they are one with Him. Let's love each other and learn from one another. No one has all the answers. If we did, we would be gods. There's only one God. Yet, God reveals to all people a hidden part of Himself. God can only reveal to us what we are capable and willing to see. We must respect all the peoples of the world, because God is in them too. God has placed the seed of His love in everyone's heart. But the light of His Son, Jesus Christ, is the only light that can penetrate the shell of a darkened soul to bring forth the seed of God's love that's deep within it.

My Awakening

It was as though I had been asleep in the snow for a long winter's night
But now that I am awake, the sun is warm and bright,
And though my body has become a part of the earth,
My soul is the shell that has encrusted the seed of the universe.
Thus, every introspective breath I take moves the seed closer to the surface.
Hence it's steadily pushing itself through the earth
To eventually fulfill its purpose.

Epilogue

September 1, 1997

I have just returned home from the twenty-sixth annual Southern California Renewal in the Catholic Church (referred to as SCRC), held each year at the Anaheim Convention Center. The convention theme this year was "Behold, I stand at the Door and Knock." That statement, (Revelations 3:20) is an open invitation, from Jesus, to all of God's people, to open our hearts to Him. I came home from that convention totally renewed and alive in the spirit of Christ!

We were instructed, through workshops, that all Christians are called to evangelize. We were also told that when God commissions us, and we accept the challenges of His call, He will provide us with all the help we need to get His job done. God never promises that the job will be easy, only that we will be rewarded for our efforts. Yet the reward is not always what we expect. Maybe the only reward that we will ever receive is the helping hands that God sends into our lives to help us with the task of getting His job done. More than thirty years have passed since God called me to record the happenings in my life, which led to the writing of *Beyond the Darkness*. There were many obstacles in those past thirty years that got in the way of my progress. There would be no book, however, without these experiences. My life is not yet over. But the Holy Spirit is moving in me, pushing me now, to get this book published.

Dolly Dorsey, a dear friend, is one pair of many helping hands that God sent into my life to help me with the task of preparing this book for publication. The idea of taping my work and then getting someone else to type it, instead of continuing to type it all myself, was given to me by another friend, Jane Nesbest, from my Saint Bernardine's prayer group.

One morning after church, Jane invited me to have breakfast with her at a nearby restaurant. At breakfast, we were discussing the gifts of the Holy Spirit. I told Jane, "I believe that my special gift is communication."

Jane wholeheartedly agreed, and she asked, "So, what are you going to do with your special gift, Madelene?" I shared with her what I believed God wanted me to do with all that He was teaching me.

"But, Jane," I said, "This book is going to take me forever to write, because I am not a typist, and I have a real problem with spelling." Jane looked at me with loving eyes and a friendly smile, and said; "So, put your thoughts on tape, and let someone else type it out for you."

I responded in amazement, "That's a wonderful idea, Jane! Why did I not think of that?"

Later that day, I shared with my son Dennis what Jane had said about putting my notes for the book on tape. Dennis said nothing in response and walked out of the room. That evening, after dinner, Dennis came to me with a small tape recorder, a dozen new batteries, and six new audio tapes. He handed them to me and said, "Here, Mom! Get busy! No more excuses!"

The next day was Saturday; at 4:30 am I was awakened by an inner voice, which said, "Start recording!" With that, I got out of bed, closed the hall door to the bedrooms behind me, and went directly into the kitchen to turn on the coffeepot. From the kitchen, I looked into the living room and saw the tape recorder on the table next to my favorite chair; it was where I always sat each morning to read the Bible and to meditate on God's holy words. The night before, when Dennis had handed me the tape recorder, batteries, and tapes, I had taken them from him and put everything down on the kitchen counter. But Dennis moved had them to the table by my favorite chair, to remind me to get started. In looking back now, I must say that, next to the Holy Spirit, Dennis has been the most instrumental in pushing me to complete this book.

It took three months for me to complete the recording of my notes. Each morning I would get out of bed at whatever hour the Holy Spirit would inspire me to get up. Sometimes it was 4:00 am, at other times 5:00. I would record my notes into the tape recorder until my family started stirring, which would be around 6:30 or 7:00 am, depending on what day of the week it was. After everyone was up, I would get dressed and leave for work. After I had completed the taping of all my notes, it took another couple of months before I could decide on whom to ask to type the recorded work. Dolly Dorsey's name came to me one day when I was praying about it. I fully intended to pay Dolly for her time. But she absolutely refused to take any money from me. I had shared with her what I believed God wanted me to do with any profit from the sale of this book. Dolly said, "The time I put into the typing will be my contribution to the cause." She was then working full-time and taking night classes to become more proficient on her computer. Dolly typed verbatim from the tapes, with no corrections or punctuation. It took Dolly about two months to finish the typing. By this time it was February 1989.

The remaining task was to get the manuscript edited. I gave the print out to Noelle to read. Noelle said, "Mom, I'm moved and inspired by the written words, but you need to find someone to edit it."

I responded, "Can you help me with that?

"I will try," she said, "but you should have professional help with it. I am not skilled enough."

A week or so later, Noelle and I began to work together on the editing and correcting of the manuscript. Noelle would come over to our house once a week to do her laundry, have dinner with us, and work with me on the manuscript—Noelle was then living in her own apartment in Santa Monica. Soon after we began to work on the manuscript, it became clear that Noelle was not the right person to help me with the editing. She rearranged sentences and replaced words, which changed the whole thought structure and direction in which I intended to go. Thus, we both agreed that she was not the right person to do the editing.

By now it was June 1989, and a lot of changes were taking place in our lives. Art had reached retirement age and wanted to move out of Los Angeles. I did not want to move. We had lived in our home for thirty years. My job was in Los Angeles, and our church was in our neighborhood. I loved the mile-and-a-half walk to church every day. All our friends and family lived nearby. I loved the neighborhood and our neighbors. Also, that was the only house we had ever owned, and it was the only home our children had known. It was the place where Jesus had appeared to me. Yes! Within the walls of that house were precious memories of good and bad times for our family. Moving out of LA meant leaving behind everything that was comfortable for me.

In 1990, Art got his way! We moved into our present home in Palm Desert, California. Nonetheless, I do like it here. We made new friends through our church, and we have good neighbors. Art chose Palm Desert because his best friend, Al Rudolf, and his wife, Lillian, moved to Palm Desert four years before we did. We used to come out to visit them before our move. That's when Art fell in love with the desert. The Rudolfs were like family to us. We had become good friends' years before, when they moved into their home across the street from us in West Hills. Having them nearby did help us to settle into our new community in Palm Desert.

This place where we now live is beautiful. As a matter of fact, it reminds me of the place in one of my visions, where Jesus called me to walk with Him on a special mountain and introduced me to Peter. I believe Jesus is calling me now, as He called Peter, to bear witness to His transforming light, the only light that can transform our lives and the world around us. Jesus brought Peter into my vision to help me understand that He chose me, not because I'm smart, but because, like Peter, I have my heart in the right place.

Our good friends from LA, and our son Michael and his wife, Janet, and their family used to love to visit us out here. They came as often as they could. We are blessed, indeed, to live in such a lovely place, but the sun is not always shining here. We have had some stormy times in this place, too. The difficulties of life continue to be a daily challenge. My mother died in 1991. Noelle separated herself from us that same year. Art had encephalitis in 1992, which almost killed him. He recovered, thank God! However, his general health was affected by that illness. In 1994, we bought a golf-cart business, which was a bad investment. We lost our life savings. We had to mortgage our home to keep a roof over our heads. Nonetheless, we still thank God for all that we have. We don't always understand why bad things happen to good people, but we do know that God is in full control of our lives.

In 1995, I began the tedious job of trying to edit this book on my own. I do not have the skills of a professional writer, and at that time I still had a full-time job outside the home. Consequently, it has taken me all these years to get this far. I have often wondered why the Lord gave me such a difficult task. Yet, I know for sure that I am not the only lowly person God has called in this world to do His will. I am thinking of Saint Peter again, my new companion and encourager, the uneducated fisherman whom Jesus called to be a fisher of men. In the Bible we are told, the wisdom of God is foolishness to men. Therefore, who am I to question God's wisdom? Those of us who believe in Jesus are called to be missionaries—because we are the chosen ones! To be chosen, however, we must answer His call. Our education, race, occupation, political preference, or religious affiliations are of no importance to God. His only requirement of us is that we spend time and energy getting acquainted with Jesus. As we set aside time each day to come into the presence of God, we will grow in understanding of Jesus' love for us and all people. Then we will be able to embrace others with Christ's love, even though it may not be popular in the eyes of the world to love the unlovable.

Christians can, and will, make a difference in the world, if we stand firm for what we believe. We must never surrender to the voice of darkness. Listening to lies and giving in to the insecurities of others leads only to defeat. We instead must be the elevating and transforming power of the Christ within. That's the only power that will move others out of their own darkness and lead them into the resurrected light of Christ.

Update since September 1997—a lot has changed in my life. After all that I had related up to that point in time, I did try to get this book published, to no avail. All I got for my efforts were rejections. So I stopped trying, thinking again that it was just a foolish dream on my part to think that some publishing house might want to publish an inspirational autobiography by an unknown author. With that reasoning, I shelved it.

Since Art's battle with encephalitis in 1992, his health took a downward spiral, along with his spirit. He suffered from depression because of his failing health. He had so many different health issues, including diabetes, which made the enjoyment of life a difficult task for him. Near the end of his life, I had to quit my job so that I could take care of him. He depended on me totally. He was on oxygen 24/7 for the last ten months of his life. He died on April 22, 2004, one week before his eighty-second birthday. November of 2004 would have been our forty-ninth wedding anniversary. I'm updating this now in November of 2006; it's been two years and seven months since the Lord took Art home. I do miss him. In spite of me missing him, I'm happy knowing that he's with the Lord, where there's no more suffering.

Art knew that he was going home to the Lord before I did. In the hospital, two nights before he died, Janet, Dennis, and I were with him, just talking and laughing with him. Suddenly, he closed his eyes; put his arms and hands in the air, and, looking upward, he said, "Thank You, Lord!"

Janet asked him, "Dad, why are you thanking the Lord?"

Art answered, "He is taking me home." Art died two days later. He also told us about others things that we would be doing in our family after he was gone, and they did happen, just as he said they would. It was as though he could see into the future. But we thought that he was just hallucinating, so we listened and agreed with him. And he made us laugh. His sense of humor was in full force to the end.

In the last two plus years since Art's passing, I have kept myself very busy with church ministries. A few months before Art died; I joined a new prayer group in our church that was just forming. Each week I would go to the prayer group for an hour. That was a real blessing for me. I made new friends who were there to pray with me and for Art.

At that same time, I also got involved with Magnificat, A Ministry to Catholic Women. The Magnificat ministry is international. However, our group, Our Lady's Desert Roses, was just beginning its formation here in the desert. Donna Ross, our group's coordinator, called to invite me to their next meeting in her home. They had had two months of meetings before she called. A dear friend, Jo Vlasak, also from my Saint Bernardine's Prayer Group, told

Donna to call. When Donna telephoned me, I explained my problem with Art's failing health, thanked her for inviting me, and said, "I'm sorry, but I don't think I'll be able to join you."

Donna replied, "Pray about it, Madelene, and if you can come, we would love to have you."

The next meeting was in July 2003, at Donna's home in Palm Desert. Our son Dennis came and stayed with his Dad so that I could go. And I have been attending every meeting ever since. The reason I'm relating all this is to share my experiences with you so that you may understand the fullness of God's love. God knew that He would be taking Art home. Thus, He wanted me to be busy with spiritual friends and church ministries. That's when Our Lord took Art from me, knowing that I would not be alone. God is so good! My prayer group friends and my Magnificat sisters have been a great support for me. I would not be doing as well as I am, since Art's been gone, if they were not in my life.

My family was also compassionate to me at that time. Janet, my daughter-in-law, came whenever I needed her. Two nights before Art died, Janet stayed all night in the hospital with him so that I could get some rest. Michael had to work, so she came in his place. At that time, they lived in Lancaster, a two-hour drive from Palm Desert. But whenever I had to take Art to the hospital, Janet would insist on coming to be with me. The night Art died the whole family was at his bedside. He was at home in the care of hospice. We brought him home at noon from the hospital, and he died that evening at 8:30 pm. Mike and Janet, Candace and Carli, Dennis and I, were all with him to say our good-byes. Noelle was not with us. She did, however, come to the church on the day of his memorial Mass and then to our home for a few hours on that same day. Since the day of Art's memorial Mass, I have been in touch with Noelle through e-mails.

I'm keeping the lines of communication open. I learned that her health problems are many. In 2006, she had eye surgery in both eyes at the same time. She invited me then to come for a visit and to stay with her in her apartment while she recuperated from the eye surgery. Where she lives is a three-hour drive from Palm Desert. Before that visit with her, it had been two years since we'd been together, the last time being on the day of Art's memorial service. This was a first for Noelle, to invite me to her place.

I have been praying for Noelle's safe return to our family since her separation from us, and I've always trusted the Lord, knowing in my heart that He knows what is best for my whole family. Like our Blessed Mother, Mary, I don't always understand. And I do ask questions, yet always trusting in His perfect will for us. Because I truly believe:

"All things happen for good; to those who trust the Lord and are called according to His purpose" (Romans 8:28).

He, the Holy One of God, Christ my Savior, "Has done great things for me." He has lifted me out of the darkness of death into His glorious transforming light of life! He's there for everyone. All we have to do is to keep our eyes on Him and follow His instructions.

Although I'm doing well, I still have my moments of sorrow, when I cry. I miss Art's companionship: his warm smile, tender hugs, beautiful dancing, sense of humor, and all his unique qualities that made him so very special to me. I loved him dearly. But the memory of the person who he was and our lifetime together will always live in my heart. Art was no saint, yet there is one thing of which I'm sure: there's not another person on this earth who would ever love me as much as he did, in spite of all my imperfections. Now he is praying for me, and he is patiently waiting for me to join him in our heavenly home.

Until then, I will continue to spread the "good news." God's love is unconditional. Good or bad, He loves us and provides all our needs. Yet, sometimes we stumble in our own darkness and blame others for our deep unhappiness. Instead, we must remove the blindfold from our eyes so that we can see Jesus and follow Him into God's Heavenly Kingdom, where there's neither rejection nor loneliness. In that place of eternal bliss we will feel the warmth of God's welcoming arms around us, as we are embraced by His transforming light of love. God is Love and in Him there's no darkness.

A Dime for Every Tear!

If I had a dime for every human tear,
The world would know me as a compassionate billionaire.
Reaching humanity in its needs, the hungry I would feed.
The homeless would have a place to stay and would be comforted in every way.
These are just a few of the things, through me, Christ would do
To show the world His love is true. But where I am now
There's very little to spare;
Thus the poor and the neglected are my spirit's despair,
For the Christ who is within me,
He is Himself a part of the sorrows
And sufferings that's in every human heart.
Yet, if only we would all give just a portion of what we do have,
The Lord would be pleased, and He would no longer be sad.
For the world would be transformed from darkness and fear
Into a place where Love lives—then, as it is in heaven,
God's Kingdom on earth would appear!

Conclusion

Whoever loves me will keep my word
And my Father will love him,
And we will come to him and make our dwelling with him.

—*John 14:23*

July 5, 2009. A few of us from Our Lady's Desert Roses Magnificat Ministry went on a six-day retreat in Omaha, Nebraska, to Mother Nadine's Intercessors of the Lamb Sixteenth Annual International Conference, which was entitled "New Covenant Power." There were people from all over the world attending that conference. Each day after the talks, we were invited to go up for prayer. There were dozens of priests there, from all over our country and the world, who prayed with individuals as they went up for prayer. People were falling like flies as they received God's blessings. They were lying all over the floor on both sides of that huge auditorium.

This is referred to by those who are "charismatic" as being *slain in the spirit*. It's a total surrender to God's power. When one falls in the spirit, one is not hurt in any way. There are volunteers behind each person to gently lay him or her down. This is a blissful experience, in which one feels totally overpowered by God's unconditional love. When you are lying there in this state, sometimes it's hard to get back on your feet without help.

On the last day of that conference, we were again invited to go up for prayer, to receive from the Lord our special gift that He was holding for us. As we were standing in line waiting our turn, I said to my friend, who was in the line next to me, "This place looks like a cemetery!" I was referring to all the seemingly lifeless bodies that were lying all over the floor in front of us.

My friend, in a surprisingly timid voice, said, "Oh no!" as if she did not want to be anywhere near a cemetery!

Then I said, in reply to her, "It's okay, because we are all called to die to self."

As I went up for my blessing, the priest asked me, "What is your name?"

I answered "Madelene," and he began to pray. He said, "Heavenly Father, Madelene is here to receive her special covenant blessing." With that, I was on the floor! I don't know how long I lay there. But it did seem like a very long time. While I was lying there, immersed in God's love, a vision unfolded. I saw myself as a little girl sitting on God the Father's lap. After I had been sitting on His lap for a while, Jesus came into the picture, took hold of my hand, and walked me onto transparent steps that took us up from where our Heavenly Father was seated. We arrived at a place where there were many souls. I saw my husband, Art, my mother, Rosa, my friend Minica, and many others who were unknown to me. We were in this place for only a short period of time. Yet when I got there and saw all those I knew who had already died, I thought the Lord was telling me that it was also my time to die.

But as that thought entered my mind, we left that place, and the vision continued. We stepped out again, onto more transparent stairs, but this time they led us downward and back toward the earth. As we were on those steps, I saw the earth moving, as if we were in space looking down on it. In the middle of the earth, there was a gigantic wooden cross. When we reached the earth, we stepped out onto the top of it, next to the cross. Then the wooden cross sunk into the center of the earth as we were standing next to it. As I was observing everything that was happening all around us, Jesus was there, standing next to me, holding my hand, and I was still a little child. Then I observed a big white dove above us, on the side where the transparent stairs were that we had just descended. The dove, which represents God's Holy Spirit, had a long, white ribbon flowing out from both sides of its beak. The vision ended. I became aware again of all that was going on around me in the auditorium where I was lying on the floor. I thought then, "I should get up." But now the white dove was hovering over me, as if it wanted me to stay there a little longer. As I lay there with the dove hovering above me, I began to recall all the visions I've had throughout my life since I've been walking with the Lord (many of which I relate in other chapters of this book). I want to share with you now more about the dove with the ribbon in its beak.

One day in 1973 I was trying to clean a canvas painting, which I had previously messed up with a paintbrush that was heavily soaked in turpentine. As I moved the paintbrush over the canvas, a new picture appeared which I now call the "Mystic Veil." I refer to this veil at other times in this book. I believe that I was led to recall all those visions, and especially that painting, because of an important message, which I must share with you. After the picture appeared on that canvas, I was fascinated. As I stood back from the canvas to look at what I had painted, I could see that the veil was parted in the middle. As I looked at what was behind the opening of the veil, I saw that the colors were bright and clear. But on the outside of the veil, on the side where I was standing, the colors were distorted and all blended together. Above the veil, at the top of the picture, was a *huge* white bird, and in the beak of that bird was a white cord. The cord seemed to be attached to the veil, which separated and opened it to show the brilliant colors that were hidden behind. As I stood back to view that painting, I remembered then what Saint Paul said:

"In the same way we see and understand only a little about God now, as if we were peering at his reflection in a poor mirror, but someday we are going to see him in his completeness, face to face. Now all that I know is hazy and blurred, but then I will see everything clearly, just as clearly as God sees into my heart right now" (1 Corinthians 13:12).

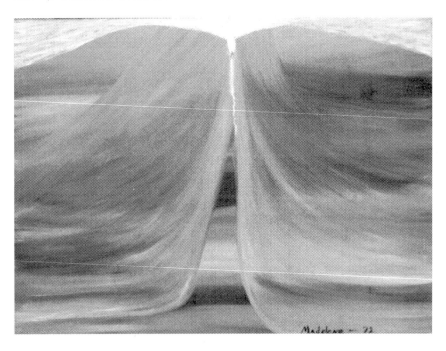

After we returned from Omaha, I came down with the flu, which kept me confined to my home for more than six weeks. Consequently, I had lots of time to reflect and meditate on all that had transpired at that conference. I recalled all the visions and took them to prayer, asking the Lord what they all meant. After weeks of journaling and listening to the Lord, while in deep prayer it was made clear to me. The Lord spoke to my heart and said: *"Madelene, you must get your book published now!"*

I answered, "But Lord, I don't know where else to go to get it published! You know that I've tried several times before, and all I got were rejections!"

He said, "Publish it yourself!"

I want to share another experience that happened in Omaha, on the day of those visions. After I was helped off the floor and was on my feet again, I went back to my seat, where my friends were waiting for me with eyes closed, as they were in prayer. I, too, closed my eyes and entered into prayer. I could hear soft music, a song of worship that was being played. But I just sat there reflecting on all that I had just experienced. I could still feel the warmth of God's love embracing me. After a while, my friends got to their feet to leave the auditorium, so I decided to do the same. When I opened my eyes and lifted my head, I saw a beautiful picture projected on the big screen on each side of the stage in front of us.

The picture was of Jesus holding a child on His lap, while a white dove hovered over His head. I sat there in my chair for a little while longer, with tears in my eyes. I said to my friends, "Look at that picture!"

They answered, "Yes, it's beautiful! Can we go to lunch now?"

I said, "Okay! But I want to talk about that picture."

At lunch, I shared with my friends all that I had experienced and seen while I was slain in the spirit. And I said, "I believe that the Lord has confirmed to me that those visions were real and that He was indeed with me in all that I experienced. The confirmation came to me through that beautiful picture."

Four months later, on the evening of my birthday, November 6, 2009, I gathered with church friends at the Capitanelli's home for a First Friday Celebration, in honor of the Sacred Heart of Jesus. Returning from the party to my own home, I got ready for bed and then decided to spend some quiet time with the Lord before retiring for the night. I wanted to learn from Him the exact meaning of all those visions that I had while lying on the floor of the auditorium in Omaha. I felt that it would be an important conclusion for the ending of this book. The following is how I interpreted what He said to me while I was in prayer.

I asked: "Lord, What does the wooden cross in the middle of the earth represent?" This was His answer to me:

The earth can only be saved through the cross. You are now standing on top of the earth. Because you are in my resurrected light, you see Me and all that I'm showing you with your spiritual eyes. You have died of the flesh on the cross with Me. Though you are in the world, you are not of the world. When I took you to that place where you saw Art and the others who have already died, I was showing you that at that moment in time you had died to self, but not yet of the body. Your body will also die eventually—but not yet, because I still need you to continue to do my work here on this earth. By publishing Beyond the Darkness, you will bear fruit to the seed of love that I placed deep within your heart a long time ago at the moment of your birth. I love you, My daughter! You are a faithful servant!

If this book was a blessing to you, buy one for a friend. All profits from the sale of *Beyond the Darkness* will be used to spread the "good news" of God's unconditional love!

The End!

What others are saying about *Beyond the Darkness*.

Madelene Balloy heard God's call: He spoke plainly to her heart and said: "Madelene, I want you to be My disciple of love." *Beyond the Darkness* explains how she continued to follow His instructions. There were many obstacles to overcome, as a working woman, wife, and mother. Yet she stayed faithful to His call. Madelene lays her heart bare throughout this book in order to exemplify in simple and humble terms that we can do all things through Christ, who strengthens us. Hers is a compelling, encouraging, and enlightening story that will touch the hearts of all who read *Beyond the Darkness*. Madelene teaches us, through her struggles, that the path to victory often comes to us as we walk with Jesus through our own pain, humility, and suffering.

Judianne Julien
Magnificat Historian
Our Lady's Desert Roses
Palm Desert, California

Magdalene shares the story of her growth in her relationship to God, inviting all to be blessed through her visions and walk with Him. Magdalene emerges from her own darkness and pain into a continual awareness of God's love for her, her family, and all people. As she continues her journey into the light of Christ, her inspiring visions reflect the growth of her personal relationship with Jesus. Magdalene relates her spiritual and deepening awareness of the tremendous gift of God's love. And all who share her journey will be blessed through her story.

Paul and Elaine Swing
Holders of Pastoral Ministry Certificate
Christ the King Seminary
Students in the Catholic Biblical Studies Program

Beyond the Darkness by Magdalene Patricia Balloy is a rich, new, and unique resource of enrichment and growth, which inspires, instructs, and challenges! Magdalene invites readers to enter into the light of Christ—the only light that leads to the higher good that permeates the inner peace of mind, body, and soul. Her narrative brings light to the truth that whatever challenges arise in our lives and in our world, our faith in God sees us through. As a wife and mother, Magdalene attests in her experiences that there's no limit to what we can accomplish and overcome when we focus on God as the source and light of all our needs.

Vicky A. Peralta, MSW, ACSW
Certified Pastoral and Social Minister

In Magdalene's book *Beyond the Darkness* there is "food for thought" for everyone: for those who have had a personal encounter with God and those who wish to have that encounter. Throughout her book, the author shares an important message: how to find God, live in His love, and share that love with others. Magdalene's writing style is straightforward and honest, giving much credibility to the events that took place in her life as described in this book.

John and Rose Vestri
RCIA Coordinators
Sacred Heart Church
Palm Desert, California

God's desire to be first in our lives is clear. As we strive to obey His calling, we meet with opposition. *Beyond the Darkness* points out Madelene's daily struggles as a wife and mother, to stay the course, as she remains faithful to her commitment to love and serve her family unconditionally; yet to surrender completely to God's desire for her, as He leads her out of her own darkness, into His resurrected light of love.

Sister Maria Eva Moreno CHS
(Community of the Holy Sprit)
Co/Chair of Magnificat Intercessory Prayer Ministry
Palm Desert, California

About the Author

Magdalene Patricia Balloy (known also as Madelene) was born on the island of Granada, British West Indies. Her childhood was one of deprivation and abuse. *Beyond the Darkness* is a chronological and inspirational record of Magdalene's life journey, beginning with an out-of-body death experience, when Jesus, in a glowing robe of pure light, appeared to her. She describes in detail all that has transpired since that phenomenal experience and relates everything of substance in her life's journey since that miraculous "born-again" occurrence. *Beyond the Darkness* relates Magdalene's personal and intimate story of life challenges, defeats, triumphs, and accomplishments. She lives in Palm Desert, California, and has two sons, one daughter, two granddaughters, and three great-grandchildren. She's a published poet and an active member of Sacred Heart Church. She volunteers on the chaplaincy team at Eisenhower Medical Center and is a chairperson for Magnificat, A Ministry to Catholic Women.

Magdalene Patricia Balloy's Previously Published Poems

A Life Worthwhile: published in the San Fernando Valley Green Sheet, 1965

Beyond the Darkness: published in Daybreak on the Land, The National Library of Poetry, 1996

My Awakening: published in A Prism of Thought, The National Library of Poetry, 1996

God is Seed in Man's Soul: published on the Internet in The National Library Poetry Hall of Fame, 1997

A Vision of Hope: published in Best Poems, The National Library of Poetry, 1997

Go for the Gold: published in Gottschalk's magazine, The Big G Retailer

All Scripture references in *Beyond the Darkness* are from:

The New American Catholic Bible, Saint Joseph Edition
And the Living Bible (Catholic) Self-Help Edition